POPLAR
MEMORIES

Life in the East End

To Mum
happy birthday
– Some light reading to
Pass the time

Danielle
26th July '15

POPLAR MEMORIES

Life in the East End

JOHN HECTOR

The History Press

Photographs appear by kind permission of Tower Hamlets Local History Library and Archives. Other illustrations are from the author's collection. Line drawings by Rosemary Whiteman.

First published by Sutton Publishing in 2002

This paperback edition first published in 2010

The History Press
The Mill, Brimscombe Port
Stroud, Gloucestershire, GL5 2QG
www.thehistorypress.co.uk

British Library Cataloguing in Publication Data.
A catalogue record for this book is available from the British Library.

ISBN 978 0 7524 5823 6

Typesetting and origination by The History Press
Printed in Great Britain
Manufacturing managed by Jellyfish Print Solutions Ltd

Contents

Memories of a Popular Man   7

Foreword & Acknowledgements   9

1. An East End Upbringing   11

2. Hospitals, Trams, Shops & Streets   31

3. May, my New Career & a Tour of the Market   50

4. The General Strike, Pubs & Street Traders   65

5. The Blitz   93

6. Friends & Neighbours   117

Poplar Methodist Church, known as Lax's, in the East India Dock Road, c. 1925. The Revd William Lax was Minister for 35 years from 1902 and Mayor of Poplar in 1918/19. He claimed to be the originator of the 'street party', organising the first to commemorate Armistice Day in 1918.

Memories of a Popular Man

JOHN ALFRED HECTOR
(25 December 1917 – 29 January 2010)

My father was a remarkable man. Surviving, as a baby, the difficulties of both infantile paralysis and meningitis (much to the amazement of the doctors, nurses and his own family) he was renowned as a little star for his courage among all the neighbours. As he grew, he met whatever challenges life sent him, and being disabled didn't stop him from enjoying the many street games the children of those times were so adept at devising. Nor did it hamper his schooling; despite spending many of his early months in various hospitals and being sent to a special school until the age of seven, his determination and hard work led him to become school captain when he joined his older brothers at Culloden Street School.

Throughout my father's working life, his strength of character, passion for hard work, ready wit and the ability to make people laugh stood him in good stead. He was respected by his bosses and co-workers alike and soon rose to become a manager at Fraser & Fraser and latterly chief buyer at Brown & Tawse of Bromley-by-Bow. He was always ready to lend a helping hand – a character trait of so many East Enders – and he enjoyed being a Rotarian and a Freemason. If it meant delivering coal in icy conditions in the depths of winter, despite his disabilities he would never think twice about the task. He wanted to help others, to be of service – as politicians have it now, 'to make a difference', I am sure that my father was doing just that many years beforehand.

As a family man we were lucky to have this strong character as our dad. He was kind, loving, firm but very fair to us girls; Shirley, Barbara and Christine (me), and he adored his beloved Lilian, our dear mother. His enthusiasm for life and all its adventures meant that he always had a tale to tell and we were a willing audience, as too were the grandchildren and great-grandchildren who followed. We all have our special memories of dad. Most of us were taught to fish and recite poetry.

My mother developed Alzheimer's disease shortly before their diamond wedding anniversary and it upset my father that the acknowledgement from Queen Elizabeth II would be lost to my mother's memory. Throughout the sad gradual decline in my mother's health, dad would always talk to her of the past; the 'good old days' of their youth, hoping, as if by some miracle, that a link would be remade in mum's mind and she would be restored to him. With her by his side and with the smallest of typewriters, ream after ream of typescript produced dad's memories of his early years in Poplar and the surrounding area. Whether he saw in my mum the fear that the loss of memory brings or, as I believe, it gave him the inspiration to record as many as he could of the wonderful times their families shared in those days, he produced a series of booklets about East End life and donated the profits to the Alzheimer's charity. He had triumphed over the adversity of mum's condition. He went on local radio to talk about the East End and his fame spread; soon he was giving talks to the WI, Good Companions and many other groups in the region. He assisted the BBC with their *Century Speaks* series and become involved with Channel 4's *Blitz Spirit* programmes. It was a good way for him to cope with the loss of his beloved Lilian, who sadly died in 2000.

Looking at dad's collection of stories one day, I happened to say that I thought they should be properly collated and published together with all the other memories he spoke of at his talks, perhaps with photographs, as a record of the time. The first edition of *Poplar Memories* was published in 2002 and my father was immensely proud of the finished book. Through its publication he made so many wonderful friends worldwide – fellow East Enders for whom dad's reminiscences matched their own personal history.

Helping dad with his work over the years has been an absolute joy for me. I never tired of hearing him telling his tales and just being in his company, as many people know, was an uplifting experience. For the last ten years of his life, despite failing eyesight and poor hearing, he embraced modern technology and learned to use a computer and voice-activated software. He also found a gift for writing, whether for publication or in the form of letters to berate officialdom on one of his many campaigns for the neighbourhood. A tireless worker for good causes, recognition of his work came in the form of his being invited to a Buckingham Palace garden party in 2007, at which he met Her Majesty. It was a marvellous achievement for him, of which we are all so proud.

Poplar Memories is an account of what life was like for my mother and father, their families and so many others like them, sometimes very hard, but always with an enduring spirit of hope. This edition of the book is a tribute to a much-loved and courageous author who passed away in January 2010 at the age of ninety-two. I thought he would be with me forever, but I will have to be content with my treasured memories and the stories of his life contained within these pages. I hope you, too, will really enjoy them.

I am so thankful and proud that I have the good fortune to be his daughter.

Bless you dad.

Christine Stanton (née Hector), 2010

Foreword &
Acknowledgements

It is hard to compile a short Foreword from my ten years of writing books, as there is so much to say; however, my first thanks must go to the many readers who have bought and read my other volumes over the past ten years and to the many local celebrities who have kindly endorsed them. The encouragement of my three daughters during that period was enormously helpful, especially while we were nursing my wife Lilian. Having lost our lovely middle daughter, Barbara, three years ago, Christine – the youngest – and Shirley have continued to provide their help and support with the present volume of *Poplar Memories*. This book is dedicated to senior citizens, to give them a record of the times and events of the borough from the ending of the terrible First World War, through to the Blitz. But I hope it will also be of great value and interest to their children and grandchildren, who sometimes smile in disbelief at the stories we have to tell. My career took me away from Poplar in the early 1930s, but I returned to work in nearby Bow, just two miles away, for the next forty-four years. I saw much of my birthplace laid to waste during the Second World War, and became determined to place on record my memories of what life was like. What Hermann Goering failed to complete, London's planners have now finished, and a virtual new city has arisen over the streets where we once played as children until the lamplighter came to light our way home to bed.

Hard times? Many years ago, I devoured Henry Mayhew's accounts of life in Victorian London. I thought, how lucky we were to be living in the time of George and Mary! Now, there are few of us left in our late eighties and early nineties who can still record our memories of those days. Perhaps film researchers, sociologists and people tracing their ancestors on the Internet will use these books as authentic records. Like 'Mayhew's London', perhaps mine will be referred to in future textbooks as 'Hector's Poplar'!

Finally, my thanks to Sutton Publishing for producing this book, to Tower Hamlets Local History Society and Library for many of the superb photographs, especially to Chris Lloyd, for his valuable help in identifying many of the locations and dates, and to Poplar folk past and present too numerous to mention.

John Hector, November 2002

The How memorial gateway to St Mary's Church, Bromley-by-Bow, was built in 1894 and still survives. The church, built in 1843 on St Leonard's Street, was destroyed during the war. It stood in the grounds of a Benedictine priory that is mentioned in Chaucer's Canterbury Tales.

1

An East End Upbringing

Contrary to evidence, the children of Poplar, where I was born, were not always playing in the streets. Most of the time they were helping in the home or running errands; if not for the parents, then for neighbours or the local shopkeepers, earning small sums of money to help the household purse. Regular errand-running was an accepted practice, and children grew up reliable and trustworthy in handling money and goods. Some shops employed older children of twelve to thirteen years old, after school, to collect orders from their wholesalers: an early operation of the 'Cash and Carry' principle. Children of this age, too, dashed out all over the East End from newsagents shops, burdened with the afternoon and City editions of the evening papers.

One job that was quite laborious was the collecting-up of bottles of Chloride of Lime from one of two depots that distributed this essential disinfectant in the neighbourhood. One, in Poplar High Street, was down a long, cobbled alley where dozens of children would form lines with bags of two or more bottles; the élite might have a two- or four-wheeled wooden cart with a number of bottles or flagons for various neighbours. It would take more than one child to pull the load up the alley to the top of the hill. The Lime water was free, and did in some small way help to keep the drains clean. Many families used it in the washtub too.

In my own family, the three younger brothers had a regular sponsor for our services, being passed on in turn as each of us left school and started 'real' work. The next brother would be inducted, and the routine carried on without interruption. Our client was the local dentist, a bachelor; apart from shopping for him, once or twice a week we journeyed to Manor Park with a small attaché case full of denture moulds made from plaster-of-paris – a two-hour journey of two buses and a half-mile walk. This earned us a shilling per trip on top of the half-crown he paid us each week for six days' worth of shopping.

Some of the girls were honoured to be chosen to take out a new baby from time to time, to wheel them up and down in prams; or perhaps an infant in a pushchair. You would see a congregation of these young nursemaids with their charges. A special girls' pastime in the spring and summer months, weather permitting, was to build grottoes from sheets of crêpe paper, fixed with bows to a wall, the pavement decorated with coloured paper, shells, postcards and any other oddments to brighten the effect, from where two or three girls would shake a tin at passers-by, calling out 'penny for the grotto, please'. Any receipts would be shared between them.

Ignoring the 'health and safety' warning not to go near the water, a favourite summer pastime of barefoot children in the 1920s was chasing the water cart.

Other girls' games included pavement skipping, a long rope held at either end by the largest children so that several others could join in the middle. Sometimes, the young mums would come out of their houses to give the girls a hand with turning and to see that fair play was exercised. Hopscotch, and 'bonce and gobs' – played sitting on a door mat – could only be played when there was no further work to be done in the home. Cricket, which the boys enjoyed, was played with a 'wicket' chalked on someone's brick wall, and a bat made by a dad from a piece of wood. Test match rules applied, but with only three or four players; more, and some might not get an innings. Football was different, being played between goalposts made from boys' caps. These would have to be rescued when horsedrawn carts and occasionally cars came by and, when opposition teams became threatening, would be placed closer together with many protests. The smallest and weakest children were usually made to go in goal. The ball, meanwhile, was made from a large bundle of newspaper, compressed and tied with string.

Leapfrog was a game for the taller boys, who could jump. The smaller boys would act as 'pillows' when the frog jump took place and anyone collapsing underneath would be called up as 'weak horses' and their team would lose. 'German cricket' was an all-year game consisting of four wooden staves, placed against a wall to form a wicket. A ball would be thrown and, if the wicket was knocked down, the thrower and his team would run away while the opposition chased them with the ball, aiming at a boy. If he was hit, they tried to eliminate the rest of the team. Meanwhile, the survivors would double back and re-erect the wicket – the 'score' was the number of wickets erected. 'Tin Can Copper' was a game enjoyed best of all when it was getting dark. An empty condensed milk tin would be thrown from a starting point such as a manhole cover, the thrower and his team would hide until one was discovered by the searchers, who would then station themselves at the manhole and declare, 'Tin Copper Charlie' or whatever the name was of the discovered child.

Whips and tops were plentiful at certain times of the year, as were peg tops, deftly wound with a cord and pulled sharply to get a good spin. Small ones made out of boxwood – 'boxers' – could be spun on the palm of your hand. Wooden hoops hit with a small stick would accompany children on errands, heavy steel hoops would be propelled with a 'skimmer', a short piece of strong wire with a hook at the end, in which the hoop would be kept spinning after a short run. These hoops could cause havoc when they caught in the live rail of the tramlines. Broken ones were mended by the blacksmith in his forge.

'Tibby cat' was a dangerous, if enjoyable game for older boys. A small oblong of wood with tapered ends was placed on the pavement and struck with some force to make it rise in the air, then dispatched with a bat along the street, the distance of the hit being paced out. Taller boys with longer strides had the advantage.

As soon as they arrived from school, however, most older boys and girls would have to light or brighten up the fire for the evening meal before their parents came home, if they both worked. Sometimes a chimney would catch fire, blanketing the neighbourhood with thick black smoke. They were rarely swept and some folk deliberately set them alight just to clear the soot and save the cost of a sweep.

Collecting cigarette cards by standing outside tobacco shops and badgering smokers was a regular pastime for the younger boys. The cards were swapped or exchanged for various offers, or used in card games – flicking or 'skating' nearest the wall, wins all. Army cap badges and regimental buttons were in good supply after the First World War, and collectable; as were foreign stamps, from which older children learned much of their geography. Fishing for sticklebacks and frogs was possible, if you were prepared to journey outside the area; Victoria Park or Beckton Road Tollgate ditch involved a long walk. You sometimes caught a fish in a net made from an old curtain, by dragging it along the stream. Barrel-organ buskers were popular, touring the pubs. One would dress as a woman and sing in a high voice, much to the amusement of the children sitting next to him on the kerb.

Children also had some devilish adventures. 'Knock-down Ginger' involved tying two neighbouring door knobs together and watching the results from hiding. Tying a piece of black thread to an empty cigarette packet or a coin, and placing the object in the path of a suspect, only to snatch it away as they bent down, was usually performed from basement steps in fading light. Police on the afternoon shift at Poplar station would march out with the sergeants in the lead; woe betide any children found up to pranks. Look-outs were posted, ready to call out when the enemy was sighted.

They were all little workers, friendly, gentle children in those days. Most had to grow up too quickly, adult heads on young shoulders. They were the salt of the earth in the next generation.

Poor and orphaned children depended on the Tabernacle, which provided a soup-and-bread kitchen service three times a week.

A group photograph of the children of the Tabernacle and helpers, 1911.

SCHOOLS

The good folk of Poplar owed a great deal to the London County Council, which controlled the running of about eighteen schools within a few square miles and ensured the education of children between the ages of five and fourteen – only a few went on to fifteen years at a couple of central grammar schools. The education was sound, and passed on by first-class teachers who accepted the production of bright pupils as a pleasure and reward for the hours of patience and devotion. Some of us must have been quite difficult to teach.

In my family we were five boys and two girls, all pupils of Culloden Street Elementary school. Each of us achieved a high standard, the youngest three following one another in becoming School Captain, under three different headmasters. Being the youngest, I can still hear the shrill whistle of the summons to the headmaster's office, wherever I was among the 220 or more pupils spread over seven classes. My eldest sister won a scholarship to the élite George Green Grammar school in the East India Dock Road.

Culloden Street had an infants' section for the five to seven-year-olds and a Senior Girls' school separate from the boys. There was a metal workshop and a woodworking section, and a fine housewifery section for the girls, all operated by first-class tutors who

Children press their pennies on The Okey Pokey Ice Cream Man. His brand was soon superseded by the 'Stop Me and Buy One' man from Wall's.

had a hard job to pass on to children who would be leaving at fourteen, all the knowledge they could in such a short time. However much or little, it was more than they would get at home. These facilities were shared by neighbouring schools, and a well-planned rota ensured that all worked smoothly across a wide range of abilities. Timewasters were given short shrift.

The imposing Victorian figure of shipbuilder and philanthropist Richard George Green gazes sternly over the local pawnbroker's shop out of picture. His dog, Hector, looks up from his feet admiringly. In the background is the King George Hall where we used to go for Saturday morning pictures. The grammar school that bore his name is nearby.

Hay Currie school in Bright Street was known for turning out very bright and well-behaved pupils. They were expected to shine under the public gaze, in the shared sections of Culloden Street, at the local swimming baths, and on Sports days. Oban Street and Bromley Hall Road pupils shared our facilities; Ricardo Street, near the Chrisp Street market, was a popular school, known for turning out good young boxers and blessed with several tough teachers of the no-nonsense type. St Leonard's Street school bordered on the Limehouse Canal; North Street and Woolmore Street schools were on the other side. No pupil in the area had a long walk from home to desk. St Paul's Road and Dingle Lane schools covered this area, while Millwall and the Isle of Dogs had East Ferry Road, Cahir Street, Glengall Road, Maria Street and Arcadia Street schools, all turning out very bright pupils.

The LCC were to be congratulated too, on their foresight in the 1920s and '30s in starting evening classes to encourage learning in leisure time. On weekdays, table tennis, dancing, art and drama could be enjoyed; above all, the children of poor families were off the streets and out of mischief.

Several scholarships were available – Christ's Hospital, Coopers' Company, Junior County and Trades Scholarship winners were awarded places at the grammar schools and higher schools until they were fifteen or older, if the families could afford it. Many bright pupils were deprived of these chances at fourteen, as their families needed the extra income to supplement the family budget. Irish Catholic families were catered for, with schools at Wade Street, St Paul's and the small church school

The preserve of the brainy few who could obtain scholarships, George Green's schools in the East India Dock Road were founded in 1828. The building seen here in about 1900 was built in 1884 as the secondary school for girls and boys.

Schoolchildren, proud parents, teachers and governors listen to the singing on Empire Day, always celebrated on 24 May. We enjoyed it mostly for the half-holiday that followed the parade.

of St Mathias in Grundy Street, which was mainly for very young children. Thomas Street Secondary school took boys and girls from other schools after they had won a scholarship place from the Trades scholarship. George Green Grammar school was the pinnacle for the district winners of the Junior County entrance exam, much to the annoyance of my mother and father, when my sister won it. They had counted on her bringing up the younger siblings, and to bring in some wages; the cost of the uniform put an additional strain on an already overstretched purse; but after a few years at George Green she rewarded them by becoming private secretary to the boss of a local engineering firm, earning a very good salary.

Discipline was tough. Memories of milk monitors shepherding us along the hall with the crates of third of a pint bottles and straws, urging the pupils to fall into line and drink up; inkwell monitors, taking the little china pots out of the desks on a Friday afternoon and down to the washroom, to dislodge the chewing gum and blotting paper that normally clogged up the little hole, and on Monday morning refilling and distributing them, ready for class. One of my Captain's chores was to assemble the boys who were on lists in the various classes as needing the cod liver oil and malt supplement to give them extra nutrition. It was a job to collect the large tins from the cookery department, each holding about 7 lb of sticky malt, to lift and twist it on the spoon and to get it in the open mouth, not down the neck; then to wash and dry the spoon, ready for the next boy. Helping the nurse to bring in lads she needed to check was another 'hurry up' job. Teeth, hands, necks, legs, eyes were quickly scanned, those wanting a second look were stood to one side, or given a note for a parent to take them along to the Medical Centre for whatever treatment the nurse felt was needed.

Monday mornings were Country Holiday Fund collection times. This was a club founded by a charity which provided a fortnight's holiday in the country once a year for children willing or able to save money towards it, the usual cost being ten shillings, payable between January and June. Some of the homes they were sent to left a lot to be desired, but it was a chance to get out of London. Memories of such holidays are fresh in my mind, I went on three – to Malvern, Maldon and Sudbury, Suffolk.

Crocodiles of children were a familiar sight, being herded along by teachers at front and rear between their schools and the swimming baths in Poplar, or the open-air baths at Violet Road, or Millwall Park in the summertime. Cricket practice was held on an asphalt area on Glaucus Street, surrounded by a high wire fence. It was a facility shared by all the local schools; Essex county cricket festivals were then a popular summer attraction. Borough track events were held at Victoria Park: teachers would implore the non-contestants to go along and cheer on Sports Day; a plea that fell on deaf ears, as it was officially a day off from school and many could not afford the train fare, which was free only to those taking part.

Being disabled, when I was very young the school board arranged for me to be transported daily to a small school with about 50 pupils, many much worse afflicted than myself, in Bromley-by-Bow, about four miles away. At the age of seven, I was assessed as being strong enough to join my brothers and one remaining sister at Culloden Street. Although unable to take part in sports, with endeavour I became Captain of the school and left at thirteen years, eleven months to enlist in the regular army of workers and wage earners, of which more later.

EAST INDIA DOCK ROAD

The East India Dock Road was one of the best-lit and most frequented walks for Poplar people. Overhead lighting and the blazing shop fronts made it a must for young and old to promenade, window-gaze, meet friends and do their courting – a great improvement on the dingy streets behind the main road. From the post office to Brunswick Road there were a great variety of shops, starting off with the jewellers and pawnbrokers, H. Neave; with the wool shop on the next corner adjacent to the Victoria Wine Company, alongside the Midland Bank at the corner of Chrisp Street market. The Poplar North London Railway ran under the road at this point, Poplar station also being the main stop for trams and buses. Next to the police station, a builders' merchant supplied most of the landlords and the tradesmen they employed to patch up the thousands of terraced houses, many of them already a century old. The tenants were hard-pressed to get any but the most serious repairs done. Two sets of wallpaper books were displayed in the store; tenants were allowed to select up to half-a-dozen rolls, at 6*d* per roll – the cheapest quality – and put it up themselves, or pay someone to do it, if they could.

The police station was a majestic building. The entrance was up six stone steps and a constable stood on duty outside, keeping an eye on the passers-by and on the traffic.

The two-storey Hippodrome cinema with the Aldgate tram passing, c. 1920.

People would stop to read the notices and stare at the photographs of missing persons or people found drowned in the docks nearby, with requests for information. This was seldom forthcoming: anyone foolhardy enough to identify a body at the mortuary in the High Street, if there was no next-of-kin, would be charged with the burial expenses.

A lovely bookshop, John Seager's, was next, and supplied the needs of the schools and shops with birthday cards and stationery of every type. Next door to that was the best tobacconist in the area, smelling richly of the cigarettes, cigars, and snuff, which was weighed and sold loose. Cigarettes, too, could be bought singly. A men's outfitters next door always had the latest collar styles on display. Detachable collars and cuffs meant that shirts stained with the city grime could be washed less frequently, lasting longer, and the styles were forever changing. Then came Waters's restaurant, a small eating-house with bench seats at tables, crisp, white cloths set in long rows with a gangway between for the two waitresses, who collected the orders from a hatch at the end. The local schoolteachers came here at lunchtime, as there were no canteens in the schools.

One of the newest shops on the street was Peter Pan, a babywear store with a good selection of clothing for the mums of Poplar babes and toddlers. This was a precursor of today's up-market shops; such a store had never been seen before in our part of London. The local chemist, Squire's, offered a seven- to ten-day in-house developing service for the rollfilms they sold to those affluent enough

Funeral processions were frequent events but few on the lavish scale that sent off London's most famous publican, Charlie Brown, the 'King of Limehouse' and licensee of The Railway Tavern, in June 1932.

to possess one of the new Kodak cameras, known as Box Brownies. The results were unpredictable, but a new generation of 'snappers' was nonetheless emerging. The Admiral Fried Fish shop offered a choice of eating-in or takeaway; next door, 'the tailor of tomorrow', Jack Emms stood on the corner of Ida Street. Brash new colours and styles, and the padded-shoulders look favoured by George Raft, were talking points for every family acquainted with the latest Hollywood movies. On the opposite corner was a Jewish dentist, Mo Lewis, a short, chubby man, always whistling, his sleeves rolled up his brawny arms, ready for work. He kept two caged parrots in the waiting room, partly as a distraction, but more to drown out the screams from the surgery. A bespoke tailor for Naval officers and other 'gentlemen', Wright's, was next door; and next again, the National sweetshop, brightly lit and endlessly tempting to children, undecided where and on what to spend their pocket money. The smell of the cooked meats – faggots, saveloys, brawn – and pease pudding from Coucha's was always appetising; they never seemed to close, apart from on Sundays.

CHARLIE BROWN, THE MAN THEY WILL MOURN ALL THE SEAS OVER

THE UNCROWNED KING OF LIMEHOUSE

PRICELESS TREASURES TO REMAIN WITH HIS FAMILY

ALL THE WORLD KNEW HIM

A LAST LOOK AT CHARLIE BROWN'S

CHARLIE BROWN is dead.
Soon the news will be told on the waterside at Rio and in the speak-easies by the quays of New York; it will reach the sailormen walking ashore at Colombo and Martinique and Fernando; on the bridge and in the fo'c'sle of ships

CHARLIE BROWN

on the high seas it will set the tides of memory flowing.

Charlie Brown is dead, and in the ports of the world they will say that London can never be quite the same again.

For to the sailormen Charlie Brown's tavern *was* London,

There it stands, by the gates of the West India Docks, crammed with the motliest assembly of curios and the most fantastic array of horrors; and there, walking down the narrow stairs from

"A MAN OF REMARKABLE GENEROSITY"

Magistrate's Tribute

Mr. Barrington-Ward, K.C., the magistrate at Thames police-court, spoke from the bench to-day about " the very great loss to the neighbourhood and the world in general " by the death of Charlie Brown. He added:

" I had the pleasure of his acquaintance, and the neighbourhood, in my opinion, has lost a very great benefactor. He showed remarkable generosity in very many directions.

" In this district he was a supporter of every good cause by means of his money, influence and personality; and the London Hospital, among other institutions, has lost a most loyal and faithful friend and subscriber.

" I am not putting it too high when I say that sympathy will be expressed with his relatives from all classes of people, both at home and abroad."

his rooms above the bar, was Charlie Brown himself, a thick-set little figure of a man, grizzled of hair, and smiling a welcome at you from brown eyes as guileless as a boy's.

" Just back?" said Charlie, in his quiet voice.

" This morning," you said. " From Rio."

And then, as he asked you about the voyage, his eyes would wander about the place—look into the long, bare bar at the back, where the sailors and their girls were dancing in the hot, yellow light to the heavy thumping of the piano, and into the little bar at the side, where the Eastern gods jostled each other by the wall, and Buddha serenely contemplated the skippers swapping yarns.

His Own Secret

For Charlie was proud of his collection—proud with a vanity that had something of the child in it—and if you wanted to win a place in his heart you had only to say a flattering word about it.

But somehow, though the sailormen of the world always talked about those wonders with a sort of simple awe, those things were not the real secret of the hold that Charlie Brown's had over them.

The secret was Charlie Brown himself. Charlie Brown, whose steps had been getting slow even before he fell ill months ago, but was still the same in spite of that—still the same friendly soul, in his grey flannel suit, and the shirt open at the neck, encircled by the

familiar black silk tie, loosely knotted and held in place by a big pearl pin.

What was there in this man of 73 which made him the king of Limehouse and the talk of the Seven Seas?

I think it was the honest friendliness of the man and the way he had of making you feel he had been expecting you for months. And his utter discretion, so strangely at variance with the guileless look of his eyes.

When he Ran Away to Sea

He had heard so many secrets, since he first went to Limehouse nearly 40 years ago, but he would never talk about them.

Live and let live was his motto; that, and as he once said to me, " Never do a dirty trick to anyone."

And he would always help you if you were down on your luck. And he would always be annoyed if you told anyone about it.

He didn't like talking about himself. Once, when he was in one of his rare expansive moods, he told me that he was born in Cambridge, and ran away to sea. And then, when he came back ashore, he was a baker and a boxer before he took to a tavern life, and drifted to Limehouse.

His fame? Yes, he knew all about it, and was so flattered by it as a child. Why, he said, a year or two ago he went on a tour of the Indies, and the police had to be called out to keep the crowds back !

He liked the procession of great people who journey down to the shabby length of the West India Dock-road to see him and his curios.

But somehow I always thought that, though they pleased his pride in the collection he had spent forty years in making, he breathed a sigh of relief when they had gone, and he was alone with his own people of Limehouse and the seven seas.

He was passionately loyal to his adopted kingdom of Limehouse. The way to make him angry was to assume that the novelists were right in their pictures of Limehouse—that the place was reeking with opium dens and sinister Chinese and broken blossoms. Then he'd tell you Limehouse was the most law-abiding place in London.

And he'd rub it in by adding that when he had a tavern near Piccadilly-circus he was always being robbed; but down at Limehouse nobody had ever tampered with his collection, which was worth—but he would never hazard a guess at how many thousands of pounds it was worth.

It was a sign of his feeling for Limehouse that he treasured a poem a sailor sent him—a poem roughly written on rough paper:

Dear old Limehouse,
Jolly old Limehouse,
Good old Limehouse town,
Full of jollity and frivolity,
Passing up and down:
Cabbies swearing, Bobbies glaring,
Toffs not worth a blooming brown:
But the homeliest place
In the known wide world
Is dear old Charlie Brown's!

The Real Charlie Brown

In the summer parties of tourists go down from the West End in motor coaches to shudder deliciously at the dark allure of Pennyfields and Limehouse Causeway, and they always called at Charlie Brown's.

But Charlie, though he was always

polite to them, felt deep down in the heart of him the same resentment that was felt by the people of Chinatown. To him, as to them, the people in the motor-coaches, imagining mystery and danger in the respectable little houses, were barbarians.

" The Chinese sinister !" he would grunt.

And then he would laugh a scornful laugh.

To me, as to him, those tourists tiptoeing into the bar were far more strange than the skulls and the sharks' jaws and the daggers and the savage swords.

The dancers on the bare floor—the big blond Norwegian and the feverishly pretty girl, the two girls from the slums dancing together with a grace that Mayfair might envy, while the cloth-caped man at the piano strummed away with a cigarette drooping from the corner of his mouth—the Lascars talking softly together in their own tongue, the Argentine sailor pulling a ten-pound note from under his jersey (and how Charlie Brown loved to say that in the West End that note would be stolen from the man in five minutes, whereas in Limehouse it was safe !) —all that was the real Charlie Brown's.

And the tourists were the interlopers, the strangers.

But if you wanted to see his collection Charlie didn't mind who you were. He would lead you up the narrow stairs to the cream of them.

The Ivory Princess

The flick of a switch, and the lamp poured its light from under the orange-yellow shade upon Ming vases 2,500 years old, and an ivory princess in a jewelled robe, as lovely and as inscrutable as when she was fashioned eight centuries ago, and upon jostling ranks of queer and precious things.

And Charlie Brown would look around at them with a transparent pride, like a child looking at his toys.

How did he get them? Charlie never made any mystery about it. He bought most of them, like any other collector—through agents in London. He decided what he wanted, wrote a cheque for it, and that was that.

* * *

And what will happen to Charlie Brown's now—and his Collection?

They will stay in the family.

Charlie Brown will be buried on Thursday. As the earth is strewn upon him the thoughts of sailormen the world over will be with him. J. A. J.

CHARLIE BROWN DEAD

WORLD'S MOST FAMOUS PUBLICAN

The world's most famous publican is dead.

Charlie Brown, of West India Dock-road—the man with the most wonderful museum of curios which any private collector ever assembled—died in his Limehouse tavern yesterday.

Kings, queens, emperors, princes,

Wiffen's was a studio photographer's. His work was always worth stopping to look at, mounted in a glass case in the window. Every subject posed in the same chair, before the same backdrop. A watch repairer had the basement; in his window was a little doll swinging up and down, attached to the pendulum of a clock that always showed the correct time.

The coach station had blackboards outside, chalked with details of the day trips on offer, their times and prices – racecourses being popular destinations throughout the year. In the summer, and at holiday times, there were trips to the seaside. Noisily clattering and grinding next door, engineers McWhirther Roberts made galleys and ventilators for the ships in the docks. Some of the streets had electricity supplied by the Fixed Price Electric Company. You paid by the week, per fitting, and the firm sold its own, very low-wattage bulbs, that would only fit their fittings. This was a boon to many households still using gas mantles, or even oil lamps.

Abelsom's the chemist was also along this parade, close to Mr Court, who had a large printing press. It was a pleasure to watch him working, assembling all the loose type in the frames and starting up the antiquated press, the sheets of paper churning out still damp with printer's ink. The next shop had rack upon rack of suits and coats on parade, waiting for another kind of press, a Hoffman press with a padded top, that came down hard on the jackets and trousers that were then hung up, still steaming, to dry. There was no dry cleaning then, but a suit well-steamed and pressed was just the job for a wedding, funeral or a night out with the girlfriend. The Commercial Gas Company showroom was always well-lit, warm and inviting on dark winter days. It was a sight to see the shining rows of new model gas cookers, all enamelled – a huge improvement on the old iron ranges in the majority of the houses in the back streets, that were such a chore to clean.

Granditers, another menswear shop, always had a selection of smart styles for the younger man headed 'up West'. Marks, the famous baker, displayed delicious loaves, cakes and wedding-cakes in glass cases, ready for the bride and her mother to inspect. Freshly baked, the tasty milk loaves and cream cakes gave off an aroma you could detect while still yards from the shop doorway. Another memorable smell came from Cardosi's, the coffee shop that never seemed to close. This was a great meeting place for dockers and tram drivers at the end of their route; also for the many less savoury characters who traded goods that had 'fallen off the back of a lorry' or mysteriously gone absent from the dock cargo.

On the opposite side of the East India Dock Road, by the entrance to the Blackwall Tunnel, was a smaller parade of shops, among them the cut-price sweet shop, Karamels, offering savings of 3–4d off popular brands, and chunks of solid chocolate, broken to order by an assistant with a huge pair of tongs. The local eel and pie shop, Shaklady's, was a godsend for late workers and patrons of the nearby Grand cinema, to eat in or take away for supper, conveniently situated next to the tram stop. And, further along, you came to Eaton's, the 'one and only oil shop', that sold everything for the DIY decorator. There was always a display outside of two-gallon buckets, each painted a different colour – this was in the days before colour swatch cards – and you pointed the brown-coated assistant to the one you wanted made up. Balbe's, the top-grade hairdressers for men and women, discreetly displayed a variety of contraceptive devices beneath the bottles of Anzora Hair Lotion, Pears' Brilliantine, hairnets and tongs. 'Something for the weekend, Sir?'

PARKS AND GARDENS

The London County Council and their forerunners did an excellent job of laying out the East India Dock Road along the mile or so from the Iron Bridge at the border of Canning Town, up to where it joins Commercial Road, gateway to the City of London. Everything anyone could want was there, including a hospital, three churches, two grammar schools, four cinemas, the Board of Trade offices and, between the fine, large houses, all carefully sited, were no fewer than three parks or 'recreation grounds'.

Tunnel Avenue park was, as its name suggests, close to the Dock Road wall and the Blackwall Tunnel; a narrow, well-tended area with a lower level set aside for children. A long walkway led on to Blackwall pier, a pleasant walk on a fine day, where you came upon an excellent view of a bend in the river beside ancient steps for small craft to tie up when permitted. The walk ended at the railway station, serving travellers to and from the upper reaches of the river.

The neatly laid-out flower beds of All Saints' Church gardens were a welcome retreat from the hustle and bustle of the East India Dock Road. Jewish folk attending the popular synagogue would congregate in the gardens, by the side entrance. Gates in the distance led to the large houses and surgeries of the local 'panel doctors', as they were called then; GPs now, I suppose. The gardens were most popular at weekends when couples getting married would pose for photographs with their guests after the service; a happy and memorable event, especially when a peal of bells had been paid for, for the crowd of wellwishers gawping through the park railings.

Children paddling in Victoria Park: an occasional treat for the author and family at Easter, Whitsun or on someone's birthday.
(Photograph courtesy of Sam Vincent)

The small playground in Newby Place, although listed as a park, was in fact an enclosed area for children, close to the East India Dock Road. There were swings, roundabouts and slides to keep offspring occupied under the supervision of a well-bribed elder sister, while Mum went off shopping in nearby Chrisp Street. But the 'Jewel in the Crown' of Poplar parks was surely the Recreation Ground. On entering the gates, your attention was immediately drawn to the lovely angel statue, erected in memory of the little children from North Street school, killed in a Zeppelin raid during the First World War. Their names are engraved on the base and can still be seen today. There were tennis courts for dedicated players, oblivious to the taunts and stares of passers-by. The floral gardens were cheerfully immaculate, and supplied from their own greenhouse. An old dear supervised the children's play area from her eyrie in a wooden hut. Several generations of us knew her only as Miss Taylor, and she kept a small cane handy for quickly settling any disputes over swing ownership.

The Bowls Club were ensconced on an excellent green at the far end of the ground. It was a grand spot to sit and observe the talent and skill of the locals. This and all of the parks were supervised, and a high standard of care was always maintained by the park-keepers. Millwall Park, finally, was the gardens leading to the pedestrian tunnel under the Thames near Cubitt Town, and gave a wonderful view of the river and the magnificent National Maritime College on the far bank. Poplar residents were proud of their green spaces, which were such a boon to mums when the long school holidays were upon them.

ENTERTAINMENT

In the days before the television invaded people's living rooms, entertainment in the homes of Poplar, as elsewhere, consisted probably of a wind-up 78rpm gramophone with sharpened wood or steel needles in a tray next to the curiously jointed playing arm; a piano, which might be found in the front rooms or parlours of the aspiring middle classes, few of whom, if any, could play it; and an early form of wireless known as a crystal set, with a primitive valve or 'cat's whisker', whose pair of headphones could be split so that two people could listen while the rest of the family sat in impotent silence. At party time, a piano player would be imported from another street, or an invited guest would suddenly reveal hidden talents, and a sing-song would ensue.

From these modest home comforts, leisure sights were then fixed on the Picture Palaces, or cinemas as they came to be called. The Pavilion, in the East India Dock Road, was the first in the district to offer talking pictures, and long queues formed to see and hear Al Jolson in *The Singing Fool*, with not a dry eye in the house during his famous rendition of 'Sonny Boy'. Gaining admission was a challenge, with a commissionaire to keep the lines in order and now and again announce that there was 'Standing room only in the sixpenny seats' while the more expensive ninepenny seats were always available. Having succeeded in gaining a seat, and they were very comfortable, many in the audience would stay and see the film through twice. Peanut vendors and buskers gleaned a living from the captive audience. Next door was the well-known sarsaparilla shop with, outside, a red-painted stall with barrels and taps ready to dispense this thirst-quenching and doubtless medicinal liquid to cinema patrons.

Like the Pavilion, the Grand in Tunnel Avenue, next to the Blackwall Tunnel, was a single-storey building with a sloping floor whose gradient hastened you to your seat. People kept exiting annoyingly by the push-bar doors, letting in both daylight across the front of the screen, and pals of the youths inside, hoping to gain free admission. Hearing the loud protests from the courting couples lit up by these sudden interruptions, the usherette or manager would rush to close the offending door and evict the freeloader. At the back of these cinemas, the standing-room-only patrons would watch patiently, resting on a brass rail, until the usherette came along the line with the welcome words 'two singles, or 'one double seat' and then you followed her torch along the aisle. People were always changing seats to avoid a fat lady or a giant with a large hat obscuring your view, and hissing at one another to keep quiet.

On the corner of Stainsby Road and East India Dock Road was a two-storey cinema, the Hippodrome. You entered the gallery via the stone steps in Stainsby Road, the pay box being let into the wall about three flights up. The staircase usually reeked of carbolic. Customers for the dearer stalls seats were allowed through the main entrance, past the publicity 'stills' of bygone stars and details of the coming

The Grand Palace Picture Theatre stood opposite the Blackwall Tunnel next to The Volunteer pub.

attractions. Up in the gallery, the seats were of the tip-up wooden variety, about twelve rows, from where missiles and other detritus could be showered on the less fortunate audience who occupied the plush seats, directly below.

The Gaiety was near the Hippodrome but a much smaller cinema, single-storey, and specialised in matinée programmes, much preferred by the older folk because of the tea interval. For children, St George's Hall near Chrisp Street market provided a Saturday morning showing with a single price of twopence. Several hundred children shouting at the villains and cheering on the cavalry could be heard over a great distance.

The Tabernacle in Brunswick Road was a church mission hall that offered children a restricted weekly showing on a Thursday afternoon, for one penny. Rather old-fashioned, it showed mainly magic lantern slides; but the regular Felix the Cat cartoon went down better with the children, who all joined in singing 'Felix Kept on Walking'. At the end of Poplar High Street was a low-grade, single-storey fleapit with a corrugated iron roof and wooden benches bolted to the floor, optimistically named the Ideal Cinema. Lascars from the ships in the West India Dock, Chinese from Pennyfields and other strangers comprised the best part of the audience; you never knew the nationality of the person sitting next to you.

Then there was the music hall. Poplar boasted only one, but what a one! The famous Queen's Theatre in the High Street was the launchpad for many well-known stars of the era. Pictures of Gracie Fields and her then partner and agent, Archie Pitt, and many others adorned the foyer. Bills were posted all over the district, listing the full variety programme; inside the theatre, the acts were displayed in lighted frames, with the top of the bill appearing about halfway through, by which time the audience would have warmed up enough to meet their expectations of applause. Outside, a hot potato and chestnut stall did a roaring trade on Friday nights, after people had been paid their wages. Every year after Christmas, for many years, the theatre was hired out for a pantomime, when hundreds of children each received a special treat, a pink and white marzipan fish, with a chocolate stripe on its back – courtesy of Clarnico, the local sweet factory.

Venturing out of the neighbourhood, a special night out was to the ultra-modern Troxy Cinema in Commercial Road, Stepney. As well as the pick of the latest film releases there was a theatre organ that rose magnificently out of the orchestra pit into the floodlights and played the hit tunes of the day while the audience were taking their seats, and it appeared again during the interval. On Friday and Saturday nights there would be a guest live act, such as the enormously popular sand-dancers Wilson, Keppel and Betty. I can still smell the perfume the management sprayed everywhere in the theatre, making an evening in its warm, enfolding comfort seem even more magical.

PARADES

On Sunday mornings the streets would be enlivened by the Boy Scouts, marching in their smart uniforms under the controlling direction of the Scoutmaster. Rivalling them would be the Boys' Brigade with their pillbox hats, some with a small pouch at their hip, hung on a white webbing belt. The Poplar Hospital carnival was one of the most enjoyable, so many young doctors, students, nurses, orderlies and volunteers willing to help raise funds for the welfare of the patients and staff. The main source of income came from the shipping lines who sponsored the hospital wards, and from the lightermen who plied their trade on the Thames; together, they were responsible for supplying many of the patients, too! I spent some time as one myself.

On Saints' days there were Catholic processions, not much to the liking of the Protestants. Four bearers shouldered the Virgin and child, another three carried the Crucifixion. The little girls were dressed all in white and swung incense burners, which brought colour and drama to the whole day. The hymns and solemn music echoed for a long time as the column wound its way along the roads. Devout Catholics would put out little shrines, to be blessed by the priest. These made a nice scene in the evening, with their candles burning in the windows. On Armistice Day, the ships' sirens signalled the start of the two minutes' silence at 11 a.m. It was something you never forgot. Now and then, 'The Last Post' would be heard and the factory hooters sounded and life started again.

The Oxford v. Cambridge Boat Race was another occasion for public display. Even the poor people of Poplar, few if any of whom would ever win a place at one of those exalted universities, really did enter into the competitive spirit, with families dividing into Light Blue and Dark Blue supporters, wearing their coloured ribbons. On the day, hawkers would take up pitches in the market, selling light and dark blue rosettes and celluloid dolls from boards mounted on wooden poles. They all charged exactly the same prices. The result of the race would not be known until later in the evening, by word of mouth, and was confirmed on Sunday morning by a headline on the newsagent's hoarding. Not many people had radios, and few in Poplar even read newspapers in those days.

2

Hospitals, Trams, Shops & Streets

A densely populated area like Poplar, with deep poverty existing alongside heavy industry and a bustling commercial docks area, was bound to put a strain on the doctors, hospitals and health visitors who served it. The Poplar Hospital for Accidents, its correct name, was perfectly sited opposite the East India Dock gate to deal with the medical emergencies that were always occurring in the busy East India, West India and Millwall docks. The long, polished wooden forms on which you sat patiently waiting your turn were filled with casualties from among the

St Katherine's Maternity and Child Welfare Clinic, Brunswick Road, c. 1935. In 1921 the author received ultra-violet ray treatment for his paralysed arm and leg but states that it brought little benefit other than a nice tan. The building on the left was Bromley Library. The clinic was slightly bomb-damaged and was demolished in 1952.

The author had two six-month spells as a baby and teenager here in the Poplar Hospital. Founded in the East India Dock Road in 1855 for the casualties of maritime and dockland accidents, it was sponsored by the big shipping lines and closed in 1975.

ships' crews, dockers and stevedores, as well as with the borough's own 'accidents'; including me, twice: aged eighteen months after a major accident at home, and again at fourteen, when a near-fatal accident put me in their care for over four months!

More serious emergencies would arrive by ambulance at one of the side entrances. The reception area was open twenty-four hours a day. The blue-uniformed nurses and sisters were firm, efficient, reassuring, sympathetic and experienced in dealing with the whole spectrum of human misery, from birth to death. Above the ground floor, the wards were named after the shipping lines that had originally sponsored them: Ellerman, Shaw Saville and Cunard, to name a few. Sailors of all nationalities were treated, the language barrier being an added difficulty for the staff. Patients on the mend would sit in the open on the roadside balconies outside the wards and chat to the passers-by, often an efficient method of transmitting a message to friends and family.

St Andrew's Hospital, on the border of Poplar and Bromley-by-Bow, carried a huge weight of the medically ill population. As well as accident cases it had a busy maternity wing; while among those who were brought in by ambulance, wrapped in long, red blankets, might well be patients with infectious diseases; TB, typhus and scarlet fever were rife. Cases would be rapidly diagnosed and sent out of the borough to special isolation hospitals. Visiting arrangements were odd but unavoidable. The hospital layout consisted of a very long corridor on two floors – wards led off on either side, and the offices, nurses' quarters and operating theatres were all adjacent. But the intake area was very small; at visiting time, in all weathers, hundreds of anxious

St Andrew's Hospital, Devons Road, Bromley-by-Bow, c. 1934. The building was opened in 1871 as the Poplar and Stepney Sick Asylum for workhouse inmates requiring medical attention, of what quality is not recorded. The name was changed in 1920.

family and friends stood outside waiting for the gatekeeper to let them in. On the word, the sound of this army of tramping feet would filter into the wards, and patients would know their loved ones were coming. Sometimes, however, the wards themselves would be locked for administrative reasons and precious minutes lost. When the time came to leave, a bell sounded, and that was it, out! No more than two persons were allowed at the bedside at any time, so a lot of waiting around was involved.

Before 1946 and the arrival of the National Health Service, you were asked to pay if you could. The lady almoner would see relatives in her office, but payment was not compulsory. Hospital Saving Association members were on a sort of private insurance and benefited from 'free' treatment. Investing in a green voucher each week for a few pennies took a lot of weight off a breadwinner's mind.

The treatment centre in East India Dock Road was really a large house. The rooms were converted into specialist areas for children sent by the visiting nurses at the local schools. Ears, noses and throats one day, eyes another. Any cuts or sores were treated on the spot and the patient sent back. Undernourished children, and those considered poorly, were weighed and examined by a small panel of doctors. If it was more than

A view across the junction to Poplar Hospital, taken in about 1950. The building was demolished in 1981/2.

just feeding up they needed, they were referred to the Children's Hospital outside the borough. A long line of mothers and children formed outside in all weathers, waiting for the doors to open. The disinfectant and ether smells seemed to cling to your clothes afterwards – for days, sometimes.

The Little Sisters had a small convent at the top of Bazelly Street. Run by some lovely nuns, it was there to help poor families, sick or injured, or those needing maternity care. As a crippled lad I tried to run with the other children and would trip up in the potholed side streets, my poor knees constantly cut and scarred. Mother would wash the injury and tie it with a rag, then, armed with a few coppers for the offertory box, I would be taken to the green-painted door, usually by an elder brother, ring the bell, and be shown into a spotlessly clean, white room. A white-uniformed nun would come in and greet us with a smile to bathe and dress my wound with Peroxide. Stiffly bandaged, I would emerge tearful – because it stung, and because I was unable to play with my 'gang'. If it didn't heal, I was to go back in two days, I was told. Those ladies were like angels to us and many other families in Poplar.

TRAMS, BUSES AND TRAINS

Although there were very few private cars, Poplar in the 1920s was well-served for transport. Trams, buses and trains took thousands of workers out of the borough on the six working days of the week and brought them back in the evenings. But the seventh day was almost as busy, on reduced schedules. The tram service from the border with West Ham was at Abbot's Road and from here the service ran to Aldgate or Bloomsbury. It was an excellent service and the workers made a great rush in the early mornings to obtain a workman's ticket, a valuable saving.

The London County Council, who owned the service, knew how to move large numbers quickly and cheaply. A one-shilling-all-day ticket – sixpence for under-fourteens – took you all over the capital on a network of trams. This was a boon during the holidays. No one was allowed on at the terminuses until the change-round operation was complete. This involved the reversal of the under-bogey and the careful manipulation of the live overhead conductor pole, and the flipping back of the seatbacks to give passengers a forward view. One major drawback of tram travel was that you could not alight between stops – the traffic behind would not stop for you, it being difficult to stop a pair of heavy dray horses pulling a load quickly. The iron-banded wheels would go into a long, sideways skid, and the cart would demolish everything in its path, including you.

A view of the East India Dock Road, where the Aldgate tram is picking up passengers outside Poplar station on the North London Railway. The tramlines were something of a hazard for horse-drawn vehicles like the one seen here. (© Ed Richardson)

Trams in Whitechapel High Street, 1932. Gardiner's department store is on the right.

The buses of the London General Omnibus Company were fitted with solid rubber tyres and were nicknamed 'boneshakers'. They ran services to all points of the compass: to Wanstead and Dagenham in the east, Paddington and Marylebone in the west, Brixton and Blackheath in the south, Hackney and Stoke Newington in the north. The LGOC had serious competitors, known as 'the pirates'. Atlas was one, a notorious bus service that poached passengers along one of the more lucrative routes into the City. Always a few coppers cheaper, they got you there quicker. They stopped only where passengers wanted them to, and you had to be quick getting off as the drivers were on a time rate. They and the conductors played up the 'pirate' image by wearing their peaked caps at a jaunty angle. Chocolate-coloured Atlas buses were frequently to be seen hurtling past the sober red of the LGOC buses.

The North London Railway was a neat outfit that carried a few passengers going out of the area not covered by the bus and tram routes. South Bromley, Victoria Park and Hackney Wick were all covered and factories in those areas found the railway useful for carrying goods traffic. Schoolchildren who were transported to Victoria Park on Sports Days – for free if they were participating – will remember the delicious Nestlé chocolate bars that could be seen behind the glass front of the vending machine there; one good thump when the porter wasn't looking might deliver an extra one free.

Outside the railway station in West India Dock Road, the horse bus served Millwall and one side of Cubitt Town, bringing the foreign seamen off the boats to sample the 'fleshpots' of Poplar!

A long-forgotten service that Poplar enjoyed was the famous Carter Paterson Parcel Delivery Service. These green collection vans ran a unique service to many parts of the kingdom. If you lived on a delivery route, you placed the CP card in your window and they would collect, weigh your parcel, check the destination address and charge you the delivery fee from a tariff. You were issued a receipt and away the goods would go, via their main depot in Goswell Street, Clerkenwell, to every part of the country.

Most deliveries were still by horse and cart, with two or more dray horses pulling sometimes very heavy loads. A wide range of goods was carried, and with the large number of pubs in Poplar, brewers Mann's, Crossman, Whitbread and Courage made daily deliveries of beer barrels and crates of bottles direct to the cellars, whose doors opened at pavement level. The carter would lower the barrels down the ramp on ropes, while the horses stood quietly nosing in the feed bags strapped to their heads. Steam-powered vehicles were also around, brightly painted traction engines made by Foden's polluting the air, belching clouds of smoke from the newly stacked furnace until, with a puff of steam and a cheery hoot, they rumbled on their way.

Albert Coe, Grover and Beattie, the familiar coal merchants of Poplar, were a hardworking lot. They had to cover every street in the borough; while, now and then, an interloper would appear, selling a dubious type of coal at a lower price. A lot was unburnable, or just fine sweepings known as 'nutty slack'. A few shops stocked bags

A more modern 'Vulcan' bus outside the Railway Tavern with, on the open top deck, a party of excursionists, probably on their way to Southend, at four hours about the longest journey they would have made in those days on solid rubber tyres.

Grove Road and the Great Eastern Railway bridge and station.

of coke, coal with the gas extracted, which would be collected from one of the three gasworks in Poplar, Bow and Greenwich. The shopkeepers could be seen pushing these bags on their market barrows, heavy loads for such a small return.

The Council, too, was a carrier, its open-topped dustcarts always on the move through the streets. A small army of dustmen lifted the rubbish from the battered bins that had mostly lost their lids, blown off in the wind or been 'borrowed'. The road sweepers attached to this cleaning brigade had little, three-wheeled, open carts. Armed with a big shovel and broom they would sweep the pavements and unblock the gutters. This meant demolishing the dams so carefully constructed by boys to float an armada of matchsticks or other wooden craft that ended up as sunken submarines. During hot and, occasionally, drought spells, the water cart would be trundled out to spray the streets and keep the noxious dust down. To protect the public against the small amount of disinfectant added, it bore a warning sign – Danger, Do Not Drink This Water. Naturally, this entertainment delighted the neighbourhood children, who would splash about gaily in the spray of water, shoes tied around their necks, as the horse slowly pulled the tanker along.

SHOPS

How the local shops used to help mothers to resolve family problems at mealtimes is not something you read much about; yet shopkeepers must have saved many a marriage that could otherwise have run into serious trouble. *Open All Hours*, the title of a Ronnie Barker show, was an apt description of the shops in Poplar then, and, of course, throughout the East End of London. The goods they stocked were the stuff of legend, are mostly unobtainable today and, if they didn't stock them, most shopkeepers would be only too delighted to get things for you, often at short notice. A number of shops are illustrated in the following pages. As a regular 'runner of errands' for my Mum and our neighbours, I had a good idea of who stocked what. Of course, there were few price-cutting 'special offers' in those days, and a good deal of borrowing of various commodities went on between one shop and another nearby.

Unlike modern, impersonal supermarkets, the role shops played in the community was important and varied. They would take a telephone message in times of illness, bereavement or childbirth. All kinds of messages could be passed on to their best customers and news exchanged. Young children would be casually employed on short journeys, collecting and delivering goods from other stores to assist in the prompt delivery of orders; and lifts given.

For the poorest people in the East End, food could often only be bought when daily wages were paid. Casual workers formed most of the population of every street, particularly just after the First World War. Most of the families were young; few children were old enough to work and earn a small wage. Consequently, 'the slate', sometimes known as 'on the book', was a rough and ready form of credit which enabled many a family to feed itself. The shopkeeper had to rely on the honesty of his customers to pay part, if not all, of their monthly bill before starting a fresh slate or page. Inevitably, debts were incurred, and in extreme cases the borrowers would be

A busy street scene with shoppers outside Fielding's stationers, Watney Street.

unable to get any further credit. Then they would approach another shop and plead for help, relying on the generosity of the shopkeeper to feed their family.

Running an errand for a neighbour, I remember once being given a note to take to the shop, requesting some items for dinner. This was handed back to me with a message to tell the lady there were three weeks' bills to be cleared before the shop would supply any further items. My mother was cross with the sender. Why didn't she send one of her own children, or go herself to plead for credit? Being disabled myself, I felt the shopkeeper might have shown me a bit more sympathy. But it was a sad, and not uncommon episode.

The journey into these shops was an education. I used to read the greeting cards, hanging in rows on hooks on the ceiling. There were hairpins in shiny paper rolls and hair slides of many colours; flypapers; Melrose for chilblains; Carter's Little Liver Pills; Beecham's Pills in little round, mysterious boxes, each containing a twisted piece of paper with two or three pills; Union Jack corn paste; one-inch bandages in blue paper; Ex-Lax chocolate and 'worm cakes' kept neatly by the side of the till. At the toiletries end of the counter were Lifebuoy soap, Sunlight and Carbosil – an early method of softening washing water; there was Robin Starch in little square boxes with a pretty robin, and Reckitt's Blue bags, packets of soda and rows of nicely turned, smooth wooden clothes pegs that lasted longer than the ones the gypsies hawked 'on the knock', although they were cheaper.

Then, the food counter, with its conical blue paper bags ready to accept brown sugar, the only type available before the granulated version appeared, and tins of

Lyle's Golden Syrup, with the lazy lion fast asleep. I always wondered why he wasn't roaring! There was treacle, which we never bought, and rows of stone jars of jam and marmalade, with the famous Robertson's Golliwog, now politically incorrect. There was tea in penny packets, always a best-seller to the factory workers, and quarter-pound bags of Brooke Bond, Lyons, or – a name that always tickled me – Mazawattee tea. The name was signwritten on the delivery van that brought it. The cheese counter, too, with its wooden-handled wire cutter; rows of glass-topped tins showing the biscuits that would be bagged up round the front of the counter, the assistant reaching back to place them on the scales.

Placed conveniently at the back of the store, bundles of firewood tied with tarry string, smelling of creosote, were kept well away from the food. Some shops had a backyard where there was a paraffin dispenser with a brass tap; a little bucket hung under the tap would recycle the drips: 'waste not, want not'. The big yards were also stores for brooms: house brooms, big bristle-heads and replacement handles of all lengths and diameters, stored under cover in a round drum to keep them dry. The little corner shops always seemed so cosy and clean, they were just the front rooms of people's houses. Your entrance was announced by the little bell that tinged as you pushed the door open. Somebody would come along the passageway from the back of the house to enquire what you wanted. They had few items to sell, our nearest sold only milk, butter and cheese. New-laid eggs were sometimes available for invalids or were taken to the hospital if especially ordered (when the backyard hens were not on strike!).

There was a special shop at the bottom of Chrisp Street. This was the children's delight, Inkey's. The front room was decked out with trays of toffee flats, about one inch round and a quarter-inch thick. Next to this were rows of toffee-apples on

Devons Road, Bromley-by-Bow.

rough-cut sticks, each one shining with a clear film of toffee. The large apples often had a nice, round lump of toffee stuck on the top, which had run down while the toffee was setting, to provide an extra treat. Sweet shops, as I shall explain next, were the hub of every child's existence in the 1920s and '30s.

FARTHING, HA'PENNY, PENNY

We were blessed with no fewer than three sweetshops within a short distance of our house. What a wonderful range of sweets could be bought in those days, for a farthing, ha'penny or a penny. The boxes were always open and the contents displayed within a few inches of your eyes; none of that wasteful wrapping you get now. Magnificently flavoured toffee: treacle, creamy banana or liquorice, broken into small, chewy pieces with a toffee-hammer. There were fruit gums, American hard gums, wine gums and, of course, milk gums, sickly sweet. There was Spanish liquorice, in many forms, real sherbet dabs, with a toffee on a stick to dip in, and Barratt's sherbet fountains in the familiar cylinder with a tube of black liquorice for you to suck your sherbet through.

Mints came in many forms: extra strong, imperials, chocolate mints, mint lumps wrapped in paper; chocolate loose or in small bars for a farthing, always eaten before you got out of the door. There were Shuttleworth's chocolate squares that had to be broken with pincers and wrapped bars of Nestlé with red and silver paper which came in penny and twopenny sizes and were also available from machines on railway stations. Everyone gave the glass front a thump to see if a free bar would drop before their train came.

There were gobstoppers that changed colour with almost every lick, all sorts of candy with a liquorice insert that could be separated before devouring, stick jaw, cough candy, coconut ice, brandy balls, clove bullseyes and, of course, for the girls, Love Hearts with gooey messages. There were alphabet letters, with which toddlers could spell out words before eating them, and Fry's chocolate bars, in five sections, each with a boy's face moulded into them. We had broken rock covered in sugar and most likely softened by age, small boxes of Imps: tiny pieces of medicinal liquorice, fiery hot to taste, that would give you tummy-ache if you ate too many. There was liquorice root that you chewed till it was dry and stringy, and tiger nuts – what these were, and where they came from, never bothered me, but every now and then you would get a small stone in one, which would hurt your teeth. Presiding over it all in a poster on the wall was the Sharp's man in a bowler hat, advertising deliciously creamy toffee.

Lucky dips were a legend in the East End shops, most commonly thumbed and grubby envelopes in a small box, which, for a ha'penny, you could fish out to see if you had won anything inside. Every one a winner, prizes ranged from half an ounce to half a pound. If you were lucky enough to win the big one, news soon spread. Other children would magically appear, proclaiming their friendship and seeking to share in your prize. The envelopes would be replaced from time to time, to stop children marking them. Another Lucky Dip consisted of a ha'penny stick of rock, about five inches long. If a black spot was displayed in the middle when you broke it in half, you won the larger stick on display. I often wondered where I could hide it on the way to school.

A favourite of the smaller children was the surprise packet. Little girls loved to open them and eat the scented cashews while searching for the gold ring or packet of transfers inside. These you stuck to the back of your hand and, when dry, peeled off to reveal a perfect colour 'tattoo'. Boys preferred to spend a penny or two on a box of caps. These small gunpowder charges could be placed between two steel 'droppers', tied with string, and thrown in the air, to land with a satisfactory explosion.

Novelty sweets were also popular; liquorice bent into different shapes like pipes, pinwheels, twists and bootlaces; soft yellow bananas and pink and white marshmallows, some covered in toasted brown coconut. There were rice paper 'flying saucers' of sherbet but it was Pontefract cakes – small buttons of soft liquorice – that were my wife Lilian's favourite.

Every July, one shop put up an attractive poster encouraging children to join the Squirrel Club. This had a picture of a cute red squirrel, now almost extinct in Britain, happily surrounded by boxes of Christmas sweets ranging from one to ten shillings in price. You could collect stamps for a ha'penny or a penny, to help you save for the festive delights on show; I never did, as I feared what might happen if I lost it.

The bigger shops along the main roads were a joy. At Easter, their windows were filled with huge eggs wrapped in ribbon and silver paper with chocolates spilling out from the centre. They were surrounded by smaller boxed eggs in eggcups and mugs or just wrapped in gaudy, multi-coloured foil. The smell of chocolate wafting from these shops was heavenly. The Christmas display, with long stockings packed with goodies, also thoughtfully provided smaller stocking-items for the less well-off. One window had two-tone marzipan fish, labelled with the manufacturer's compliments: Clarnico, promising that every child who attended their pantomime at the Queen's Theatre would receive one free, along with an apple or orange donated by the market traders.

When the festive season ended, this shop had a sale and filled its window with bargain lines. They also specialised in a sweet called 'Chicken bones'; long, thin tubes of brittle toffee, they had a creamy filling and broke easily – like the equally fragile nut rock pyramids they were tricky to share with your friends!

Having older brothers and sisters meant that pocket money came my way from errands. Running messages, delivering things or collecting clothes from the cleaner's for a copper or two could be a lucrative business, but could also go wrong, especially if you delivered the message to the wrong person. When I got my cash reward a small group of followers would appear, as if from nowhere. ''ow much yer got? What yer goin' ter get?' Sometimes the shopkeeper would ask who was actually the buyer, then the rest would be turned out to stare longingly through the window, hoping I would buy a big enough bag to share. Older children in charge of smaller ones in prams would be seen supplying the child a small, coloured toffee apple, which cost a ha'penny. This invariably ended in a sticky mess but kept the young 'uns quiet.

A nearby off-licence sold sweets and boxes of chocolate. Cadbury's had a range with pictures of the king and queen on the front, with a large bow. Caley's sold bars that tasted more like wax than chocolate, but were cheaper than Terry's, Fry's or Nestlé's. This shop also sold monster penny bottles of coloured 'pop', which had to be drunk on the premises or it cost an extra penny. Toys were also sold in these shops such as clay marbles, as well as the more prized, coloured glass variety. There were also spinning tops, and 'boxers' – miniature tops made out of polished wood which lasted for years if not lost or mistreated.

ROADS AND PAVEMENTS

Borough Council workmen do not receive sufficient attention or gratitude from the public. As children, we loved the excitement and, of course, the change of scene and the disruption to daily life that came with the replacement of the pavements in our street. Some housewives proudly whitened their front doorstep and a half-circle of pavement around it, as their mums and grans had before them. This was a hard chore the young women were obliged to perform. After beating the front mat against the wall and sweeping the dust into the gutter, a large block of whitening and a wet cloth would be artistically employed, sometimes across as much as a third of the narrow pavement, forcing passers-by to walk perilously near the kerb, while Mum kept an eagle eye on her drying artwork. Once the door was closed, of course, pedestrians took no further heed and the operation was repeated the following week.

The lifting and placing of the York stone squares was a skilful but heavy job, sometimes taking two men; though usually there was one very large, heavily built man chosen for his size and weight. He would lift and drop the slabs in just the right spot on the sandy bed and, with the back of his shovel, push the edges square and in line, all along the street. When all had been laid, the sand filler would get on his hands and knees to fill in the gaps, a process that had to be repeated several times as the

Workmen replacing stone cobble setts outside the Sailors' Palace in the West India Dock Road. Russell's sheet metal merchants is seen beyond.

sand settled. Fragments of broken paving slabs made excellent sharpening stones and other tools. My father had two or three in our backyard, serving as anvils to straighten bent nails that were never thrown away, recovered from the broken boxes that mother used for kindling wood. One well-worn slab was used solely for sharpening carving knives, the stone wetted with water from an old milk tin on the shelf above. Other stones when put side-by-side formed a level surface for standing things on, such as small items to be painted.

To obtain these items, householders would be friendly towards the pavement men, and of course the publicans and shopkeepers would come forward with a glass of beer or a can of hot tea. In later years, however, the broken slabs all went back to the borough to be sold for crazy paving or hardcore. As prosperity increased, people would acquire pieces of stone or concrete flags to make paths over their muddy gardens, to the outside w.c. or the water tap; the modest charge for half-a-ton or so helped to remove the large quantities of rubble from streets that needed repairing after years of neglect by cash-strapped councils.

The road repair gangs arrived with horses and carts loaded with a tremendous variety of equipment. This included the workmen's hut, a long tunnel of half-hoops covered with sheets of striped tarpaulin, which acted as a store for all the tools, and the coke brazier, that beacon of hope for the team's survival. The hut, with its watchman in charge, would soon be organised. Scaffold-board seating was mounted on 10-gallon drums, filled with water. The men could enjoy a hot meal or a brew-up, and eat their sandwiches, which were kept wrapped in a tin on a makeshift table, under the eye of the watchman. This was their domain for the duration of the job.

The street where we lived was one of the earliest to be laid with tarmac, which proved much quieter when horsedrawn carts were delivering. Four side streets leading off this long street were our playground, as with no shops to supply they were rarely used by carters. When one of 'our' streets was being repaired it meant finding a new venue. We might be forced to trespass on other children's play areas. Sometimes it meant we could play a wider range of games; the odd member of our gang who switched sides would not be welcomed back when our street had been modernised.

There were no mechanical hand tools in those days, just hammers, forks and shovels, with wheelbarrows to take away the spoil aboard the carts that brought the new filling. This would be granite stones about two to three inches in size. After it had been spread and levelled, a huge steamroller would arrive with a cheery hoot on its whistle, smoking and clanging, to flatten the staked-out pitch. At lunchtime, the men would return to the hut and stand around the blazing coke fire. Tea would be poured from a huge teapot. The mugs already had milk added from a large Cross Brand tin punctured with several holes to make pouring easier. Then a long toasting fork would appear, and large, thick slices of bread would be toasted, to be eaten without butter.

Cotton Street. This corner, where long baulk of timber has come off a cart before an audience of curious onlookers, was obliterated in 1945 by a V2 rocket.

Old Ford, where Levere Walk was. Iron railings became largely a forgotten feature of London's finer squares and walks in the early months of the Second World War. Owens & Son was on the corner.

When work finished for the day, the tools would be cleaned and placed in the back of the hut, and the watchman would set out the heavy, round, iron base-plates with upright steel rods, on top of which were hooked the guardropes and paraffin lamps whose dim red glow warned road users of danger in the dark street. He would carefully fill the lamps, and then light his own, larger lantern, which gave him plenty of light to while away the night hours inside the hut. I struck up friendships with these lonely men. Some were not very old, a few ex-servicemen, disabled and unable to do the hard work they had been used to before the war. Now and then I would take a potato or two from Mother's basket and we would bake them, sitting around the warm brazier, listening to stories until a shout from the front door summoned me to bed.

One street nearby was still made of the old, tarred, wooden blocks and, when news spread that this was being dug up, people appeared from all over with prams, barrows and sacks, eager for free firewood. The workmen put the blocks aside and a foreman saw that everyone got their fair share. Of course, there were young 'entrepreneurs' who, for a price, offered to sell the firewood to those without transport, or who were too infirm to collect it themselves. The ancient blocks split easily, but the layer of tar and rubble that had accumulated on top was highly combustible and, unless removed, would spit stones out of the fireplace and hit the folk sitting nearby. After burning a lot of these tarry blocks you used to get chimney fires, treating the neighbourhood to a cloud of smoky soot, and mothers would have to bring in their washing.

After the steamroller had done its stuff, a team would arrive to spread the steaming tar, sacks around their waists to protect their legs. I still remember the smell. Gravel would then be pressed on to the still-hot tar with a light hand-roller. Often, mothers with babes in arms would be seen talking to the tar-boilers. There was an old wives' tale that the infants' lungs would benefit from inhaling the fumes of the hot tar. I have often wondered if it worked: there was a lot of tuberculosis in those days.

The main road through Poplar was the East India Dock Road, and every now and again this would be held up in one direction while its large granite setts were being replaced; especially where these had split or subsided and cause a horse to stumble or a cartwheel to get stuck. This heavy stone-laying was an art and the workmen real craftsmen. Over the years I watched them work, as a young man and as an adult. I came to admire the hardworking men and women who were born and bred in Poplar.

A TRIP TO THE CITY

My mother had promised me a trip to the city. We planned it for weeks and I was looking forward to the great day, which came sooner than I anticipated. I was bathed in the morning! Actually, it was just a 'top-and-tail', not like the Friday night bath, for which we all got ready, one after another, and the first ones got the hot water and the dry towel.

Dressed in my Sunday suit, off we went on the Bloomsbury tram. A long walk through the streets to Holborn brought us to a great pair of iron gates that proclaimed St Bartholomew's Hospital. It was the place you went to for all your ailments in the years before Great Ormond Street children's hospital was opened. We sat on the wooden forms for a while until my name was called, and a pretty nurse took my hand and led me to a table with a white sheet on it. She placed a cover over my suit while Mum was shown a seat in the corner. A very tall man came and looked at me, smiled, opened my mouth and put into it, something that tasted like Gibbs's tooth powder, that my sister used. There was a sharp pain, then the nurse stood me up and gave me a piece of white lint to hold over my mouth. Another nurse appeared, dressed in a dark blue uniform and a funny little hat, tied up with a bow. It reminded me of the little girl in the pram next door, but Mum did not seem so amused by what she was being told.

On the tram journey home, a big parcel beside her in a shopping bag on the floor, my mother muttered angrily to herself. I was glad of a cup of warm tea to ease my sore throat, which seemed to be swelling. Dad was busy with the daily task of shaving himself with an open razor in the small mirror beneath the gaslight. We watched in silence as he wiped the lather on the small squares of newspaper that I cut up in my spare time and threaded on a string, like the larger bundles in our outside toilet. Mother was catching up on her ironing, shoving the three flat irons back and forth on top of the hot kitchen stove, just inches from Dad's legs.

My father stropped his Krups razor, before putting it carefully away in the correct day-case, one for each day of the week, and locked it away in a drawer. Then the story all came out: how they had taken out my tonsils, and Mother was insulted because the second nurse had said that I was poorly, and weren't all six of her children, boys and girls, healthy? Father muttered in agreement and settled down to read the newspaper. The story was recounted in minute detail to every visitor, as well as to the poor woman from next door, who had only popped in to borrow something. In fact, although I was well cared-for, the youngest child of seven, I was not 'healthy': eighteen months into my life tragedy had struck. Boisterous brothers and sisters jumping about upstairs went through the old floorboards and brought down the ceiling of my mother's bedroom, where I was sleeping. I was rushed to Poplar hospital, just 400 yards away. It was a miracle, they said, that I was still alive; but I developed meningitis, causing a fluid swelling compression of the brain. A London hospital surgeon was sent for and he decided to pierce my skull in seventeen places to drain off the fluid. The results would be uncertain: brain damage or physical impairment were possible. The actual outcome was a condition known as infantile paralysis which affected my right side, and still does, eighty-two years later. It proved very useful in 1921, when my family were able to obtain food vouchers from the council; and it kept me on the Home Front during the Blitz, of which more later.

3

May, my New Career &
a Tour of the Market

My dear sister May was very deaf. An attractive blonde, eighteen years old and with a nice figure, she worked very hard and long hours in a steam laundry. May had very little time to herself, but was addicted to 'the talkies' as we called them. She was a regular patron at the Pavilion cinema nearby, and had the advantage of knowing two of the staff, the commissionaire, Mr Ferry, and his usherette daughter, who rejoiced in the name Hepzibah. These two always gave May their best attention.

Following visits to the cinema, Hollywood fashions became a magnet for May's hard-earned savings. Such styles were not to be found in Poplar. The only shop women had locally still sold whalebone stays and blue, fleece-lined knickers, described as their 'best-sellers'. The only places to get styles similar to the movie stars were in Aldgate and Petticoat Lane. Shops here obtained garments from West End stores, copied them and freely displayed them 'straight from the USA'. This was where May shopped, and I acted as her interpreter, on account of her deafness; my constant allegiance was usually rewarded with a small coin, or a promise of one. When savings allowed, on a Sunday morning, we would set off on the Number 67 tram to Aldgate. If it was raining, so much the better, as better prices could be obtained: such days were the best-selling days in the Jewish calendar. After peering in window after window at the fashions on display, ignoring the barker who always claimed at the top of his voice to have the 'biggest range in the market'– this was to intimidate his rivals – we would enter the most promising-looking store and browse the selections.

Everything had to be compared for colour, size and style. Bust and waist measurements were Greek to me at the age of ten. If she decided that she had found what she wanted, May would signal to me by placing her hands together with the two thumbs pointing upwards, before moving towards the door. This flummoxed the poor salesman, who thought a sale was getting away, and in desperation he would lower the price. May would then open her purse, so he could see she was serious, and demand a still lower price. This clinched the bargain, and she would leave the shop with her trophy in the shop's own bag, only to transfer it shortly afterwards to a plain shopping bag so no one at home would know where she had been. If there was

The author's elder sister, May, was profoundly deaf. This did not, however, stop her from visiting the cinema, where she was friends with the commissionaire's daughter, or from shopping ruthlessly for the latest fashions. She is seen here with her 'dream husband' darts champion Eddy (Monty) Doughty.

nothing she desired, May would signal me to leave first, then rise from amid the pile of try-ons and exclaim that she had to go now, in case I got lost! There was no chance of that.

Next, shoe shops were explored for the matching styles, shapes and heels that would suit her other purchases, and we sat for ages amid a growing pile of boxes until a suitable pair could be found. With another prearranged signal from May, I would note the size and style on the preferred box, and then May would sigh and remark sadly that they were not what she wanted but we might 'come back later'. The poor shop girl would have to put all the boxes away again; so that, when we did return the next week, or whenever funds permitted, she was so pleased to be asked for the 'right' pair of shoes straight away, that she was happy to accept a lower offer. On our way home, Assenheim's ice cream would be devoured triumphantly, in time for Sunday lunch.

All togged-up and out to visit friends, May was admired by a fleet of young and old alike. Some would ask if she was courting, and where had she bought her lovely dress? When May did find the man of her dreams, she could not have made a better choice; a devoted husband for life. My work as an interpreter was over, I was ten years old and unemployed, with only my memories of a beautiful, kind sister so sadly afflicted by deafness.

MOTHER'S YOUNG WAGE-EARNER

A month before my fourteenth birthday I was summoned from class by a shrill whistle to go to the Headmaster's study. Nervously passing the hall where the choir were practising for the Christmas carol service, I wondered what I had done wrong. Had I put the money for Sprackling's new cap on the Headmaster's desk, as I had been asked to? Yes, he had locked it in the cashbox in his drawer. I knocked at the door, and waited for permission to enter. This seemed to take longer than usual, but at last I went in and found a tall, fair-haired, spotty-faced young man already there. This was Bill Williams, who had left the school two years earlier and found a job. He had so impressed his boss with his progress that he had been sent back to Culloden School on a mission to find another suitable lad to fill his boots, as he was being promoted. Was I interested?

I had not yet thought about finding a job. I was more interested in my approaching birthday, which happened to fall on Christmas Day. But the Head asked me if he could trust me to keep up the good name of the school, I told him I could, and it was arranged then and there that I should go along the following day and report to Billy's boss. At worst, I thought, it would be a day bunking off school.

Outside the door, Bill explained all about the job and I anxiously prompted him, knowing that I would be thoroughly interrogated by my parents and my four brothers and two sisters well before I arrived at the offices of Messrs W.B. Bawn & Co. Ltd. At 9 o'clock the next morning, I set off for 47, West India Dock Road to meet the boss. I was shown through a noisy workshop with dozens of men and boys, all in work clothes. Some wore boiler suits, which I knew denoted their special rank. We went through a little house in the next street, Castor Street, behind the first workshop, and entered a second, which was the welding shop. Flashes of brilliant blue light were punctuated by heavy, metallic thumping noises. Bill knocked at the door of an inner office and there was my new boss, Mr Harold Hindle, a round-faced, heavily built man wearing a battered fawn trilby hat and the white, starched collar and tie that made his managerial status official.

Questions flowed thick and fast. I had to explain that I was lame owing to meningitis and infantile paralysis, although Bill had probably already told him. He gave me a writing test and some easy mental arithmetic, which I answered to his satisfaction. Much to Bill's delight, this brought an immediate offer of a job; he was keen to offload all the menial work he had been saddled with for the past two years! The wages and hours were: 10s 6d per week, 8 a.m. until 5.30 p.m., Mondays to Fridays, and 8.00 until 12.00 on Saturdays. One week's paid holiday and a review each March, with a promise of a small bonus at the end of the financial year. I was to start work the week before Christmas, if the school was happy, and would be given assistance until settled.

Mother was waiting anxiously with a cup of tea. The regular wages would help with the family's finances and she was delighted that her young 'crippled' son was off her hands and working for a living. My father was naturally full of questions, and delighted too, as he had worked with Bill Williams's dad in the docks for many years and knew him well.

The room that I had my desk in was opposite Mr Hindles's office and for a while I shared it with Bill until I knew the job reasonably well. He was moving to the main

Poplar's Brunswick Pier: a view of the London and Blackwall Railway terminus with the steamer Braemar Castle *entering East India Dock. Opened in 1840, the pier was demolished in 1947. 'Batey Kola', advertised on the kiosk, was a popular drink.*

office, the next rung on the ladder; although for many months he was back and forth across the factory seeking information from the platers' foreman or the electric arc welding foreman, whom I shared the office with. From them I learned to grow up very rapidly in the engineering world and thus, from the job of office boy, went on to become internationally known and, hopefully, respected in the steel industry.

FIRMS AND EMPLOYMENT

A large number of men and women owed their livelihood to the local firms that were founded and grew up in Poplar and the surrounding area. They were able to work close to home, saving the fare and enjoying more free time. Neighbouring Millwall was a hub of industry and activity. C. & E. Morton's Jams and Preserves was a clean, pleasant factory employing mostly young women, all neat and tidy in the overalls with which they were provided – a great contrast to the young lads who worked at Vince's Dry Battery factory in nearby Garford Street. They went through the gates at the start of every shift, nice and clean, and came out looking like 'Kentucky minstrels'. The adjacent foundry of C.W. Gill saw an endless stream of barrows going through the weighbridge, each load of scrap iron that the rag and bone men had collected being carefully checked. The furnaces spewed out columns of dark smoke when first lit.

An aerial view of the Bromley Gasworks, Bromley-by-Bow, 1920s or '30s. In the foreground is the River Lea. Built in 1873, the gasworks operated until the 1970s when coal gas was replaced by the cleaner North Sea variety. On the right of the picture two-thirds of the way up was the location of the author's offices and 'temporary home' for four years during the war.

Women loading laundry into the big washing tubs at the public washhouse in Sophia Street. The mechanical washing section was opened in May 1931. These women would earn a few pence taking these huge loads for neighbours and customers.

J. Kirkcaldy, ships' plumbers, and Houchin, electricians, were nicely placed next to the docks for taking on emergency repairs. The famous Hawkins rope mill employed highly skilled craftsmen turning out very large mooring ropes, twisting and turning the hemp expertly on the rope walkways. They also produced smaller versions, for instance for the Brixton prison hangman. John Lenanton, timber suppliers, were also ideally sited on the river. Barges could bring and unload timber from all over the world. Burrell's paint factory was close to the petrol tank makers, John Bellamy. Both firms employed skilled men for the heavy work involved, as did the bridge builders, Joseph Westwood, recognised during the Second World War more for their tank landing craft, which were launched on the Thames.

Gasometer makers Samuel Cutler were busy in the 1920s welding and repairing the huge town-gas holders that were once prominent throughout the UK, before North Sea Gas. The much-photographed Oval gasholder was maintained by them. Millwall was also the home of the ubiquitous Sterling washing mangle, known by every housewife in pre-spindrier days as an instrument of hard labour.

From the road in West India Dock could be seen the life-sized figure of a ship's helmsman, complete with wheel. This figure, the trademark of W.E. Brown, tankmakers, withstood the rigour of the war years, and is still intact, presiding over their new factory in the Eastern counties. Brown Lennox and W.E. Moore employed teams of experts, who toured the capital and its suburbs testing chains and lifting gear in factories to certify them as safe. The Factory Acts Safety First Procedure was a forerunner of today's Health and Safety legislation. One of the finest coppersmiths in London, Blundell's were kept busy by the breweries and the confectionery trade. Richards & Sons was a small, family-run business known as a fine firm of tinners. The father and four boys were always hard at work, cleaning and re-tinning hundreds of pots, pans and cauldrons for the home, export and shipping trades.

Missing the opportunity to set up in nearby Barking, Spratt's Dog Biscuits employed dozens of women, young and old; indeed, they also supplied the Armed Forces and shipping companies with 'hard tack' emergency rations for lifeboats. These were bullet-hard and lasted for years, but they saved lives. Nicer, more edible table assortments were produced at the far-famed biscuit factory nearby, where children hung around at going-home time, hoping for a few broken samples. The famous Lloyd Loom furniture was invented and made in Poplar, using a unique method of construction. Strands of thin wire tightly wound with paper were 'woven' into chairs, baskets, stools and ottomans, apparently the widest range ever produced by one furniture company. The items were spray-painted, in colours attested to by the wide range of shades apparent on the workmen's overalls after each shift. Another part of the company produced drinks crates for the brewery and soft drink trades, in an age before throwaway bottles became the norm.

The Emu Wine Co. was something of an oddity, importing Australian wine in bulk and bottling it for the UK market. Not a lot was drunk locally, Poplar folk were more your ale and bitter types. The Sun flourmill was an ancient building on the canal. Even hours of rain never seemed to shift the ghostly sheen that coated both the employees and the district when the wheels were grinding. Saul D. Harrison's rag mill was a dreary building, taking in old rags to be washed, dried and then chopped and sheared into small pieces. It produced what was known as 'prime flock' for use in the bedding and upholstery trade. This firm later imported large blocks of solid packed fibre and broke them up, beating and teasing them into bags of loose fibre filling. The employees wore masks over their mouths and eyes and were permanently covered in a reddish dust. They earned every penny of their wages doing a dirty and dangerous job few would willingly undertake.

The firm of Cairda and Rayner was world-famous in shipping circles, manufacturing desalination equipment that provided fresh drinking water for ships' crews, half an ocean away from the nearest port. Another firm where craft skills were appreciated was Bright's in Rhodeswell Road, who still made the carts and wheelbarrows used by traders all over London. These were brightly painted and carved from various woods. After rubbing down, many coats of varnish needed to be applied. The market traders' signboards with their gilt-edged lettering had their origins at Bright's. Hitchman's dairy in Kirby Street employed a small army of roundsmen, pushing their familiar three-wheeled milk floats through the streets of Poplar, a large milk churn perched in the centre of the cart. The noise of their clattering could be heard from a great distance. The milk came fresh from the stalls in the dairy yard, where the cows would be stationed and then let out to graze in some local park. 'Accidentally' leaving the lid off the churn brought the roundsman a heaven-sent bonus on rainy days.

George S. Clayton's dairy was also nearby; the company is still in business today. It was a delight to go and watch the intricate bottling plant at work. With dozens of smaller businesses and self-employed craftsmen and tradesmen, Poplar employed thousands of men and women and their skills gave us numerous products of the highest quality. These skills were handed down to the young, making Made in Poplar a trademark to be proud of.

CHRISP STREET

In my memories, I often wander through Chrisp Street market. At the East India Dock Road end, where the market begins, is Burgess's Fruit Stall, with the polished brass rails, signwritten and varnished nameboard, the prices neatly displayed. Brown paper bags, stretched over cardboard, form the price tickets that are marked with prices in Rickett's Blue, each atop its pyramid of scented fruit. Here too is the ladies' hatshop – some straw, some veiled and in a variety of colours. Not quite next door is Manzi's famous eel and pie shop, with its tanks of live eels for the shop or the passing trade and next to it, Udal Bros' shellfish stall: crabs, winkles, cockles, scallops and jellied eels, always clean and fresh-smelling of the seashore, next to the bottles of Sarson's vinegar on display. Opposite was a wonderful stall, always colourful, with flowers of every description. This was carefully created by Mrs Briggs, who made an early journey to Covent Garden, sometimes to complete a wreath order for a customer. Gallons of water were poured on the blooms to keep them fresh. Her stall was outside the True-Form shoe shop, which enabled her stall to be lit for free.

On the opposite corner with Susannah Street is the original of the famous chainstore, Burton's Tailors. Outside, the Salvation Army band plays, while Army lasses sell copies of *War Cry*. In their absence, buskers, barrel organ-grinders or even chained-up escape artists would perform – but only if there was enough in the hat.

Chrisp Street market, c. 1910. Grundy Street fruiterer, Edward Green (d. 1935) pioneered the market with his brother. When the street traders were forced out of Poplar High Street in 1878 at the request of the shopkeepers, he set up his pitch outside Oxenham's drapery store in Chrisp Street.

Facing the flower stall is a dinky little Woolworth 3*d* and 6*d* store, newly opened. A pair of slippers costing in reality a shilling were priced at 6*d* each slipper, rather than confess that anything there cost more.

Outside Woolworth on a Saturday evening, you would find a sweet stall run by a man named Goldie, on account of his two front teeth, which were solid gold. Under his flaming kerosene lamp he would mock-auction boxes of sweets and chocolates of unknown or obscure origins, knocked down at low, low prices. Moving along, we come to the market favourite, Piper's Cooked Meat shop and stall. Pease pudding, faggots, saveloys, trotters, black pudding, tripes – and the scary half-sheep's head, all steaming and a great provider of an East End supper for some late-working family. Facing this was the children's dream stall: Pearson's Home-Made Sweets, wonderful smells of cough candy, coconut ice, bull's eyes and brandy balls, displayed for all to see.

A row of three shops is occupied by Harry Neave, the big furniture and furnishings outfit. Rolls of linoleum and cheap oilcloth, chairs, perambulators and beds stand outside on the pavement, chained for security. Facing them, Oxenham's, the drapers, reminds me of Grace Brothers in *Are You Being Served?*, the assistants uniformed in black, with white collars. The cash for your purchases was put into a wooden ball with the receipt, and elevated up a wire railway to the cash desk, from where you waited for it to be returned with your change. A farthing change would come carefully wrapped in pink paper, folded with pins. All the prices were something and three farthings, never just sixpence or a shilling.

Busy little Endeans, the leather shop, is a regular trip for most families to buy shoe leather and rubber heels to mend the family's shoes; together with Blakey's protectors to try to prevent the rapid wear that children with home-made scooters, particularly, soon produce on one boot.

Between the stalls and the shops roam the street vendors, trays suspended from strings over the shoulder, displaying shoelaces, lavender bags, little white sachets of horseradish. Now and then a war veteran, perhaps blind, offers boxes of matches on his tray that you can take, or leave a copper to help. Medals – the Mons Star in particular is much in evidence and recognisable to most people. Bundles of best elastic and packets of ladies' hairpins for a penny or two help these forgotten heroes to get a bare living.

The next shop to Endeans sells a variety of shirts, underwear, ties and scarves, and loose collars with fashionably long peaks, all the rage in the 1920s and '30s. Across the street is a well-known provision merchant, Coppen's, whose assistants pride themselves on knowing dozens of their customers by name – as well as their individual requirements, bearing in mind that cost-consciousness would always endear such customers to their particular brand of service. Bacon, biscuits, cheese and eggs are among the dozens of lines stocked. Part of the counter bears a dozen or so glass-topped tins, showing the various biscuits and the price per pound. Broken biscuits are sold in bags, quality and type unknown until you unwrap them. Eggs are always handled separately and placed carefully in brown paper bags, to be carried gingerly on top of the shopping.

Further on still, are the arch-rivals of the Burgess stall, Fitch's. Despite being fully a quarter-mile apart, each was constantly sending touts and lookouts for a small fee, to report on the other's prices. Near them is the first of the fresh vegetable stalls run by the Softley family, the boys well-known in East London boxing circles, hardworking tradespeople and well-respected. The Pot Herb lady, too, was respected for her little barrow offering a selection of carrots, onions and turnips, set out on a tin tray in quantities sufficient for a local stew known as Sukie. Next comes a very large stall plastered with books, comics and magazines for every interest, mainly suspended on clothes pegs so you could browse the titles, but not the contents. This is run by the Ballard family, obliging and well-informed on most topics, and willing to procure you anything – love, crime, mystery, adventure – if not in stock.

Wallace's is a marvel for its display of china, buckets, brooms, mats and cutlery, just a few of the items on offer with a notice informing you that 'a small deposit secures'. Boots the Chemist is just a small, efficient shop on the corner of Southill Street, where a group of ladies is surrounded by a large crowd, waiting to see what items are held up from a mountain of secondhand clothes on the pavement. Hands reach for a garment 'suitable for a girl or boy of six years old' – or a small nine-year-old – at the knockdown price of 3*d*. This pavement raffle helped to clothe many a junior member of the large, impoverished families prevalent in those days.

Overlooking the market, mounted on a roof, is a very large, red teapot. Beneath it, 'Tea Pot Jones' is a master provisioner, a wholesaler supplying the market and delivering to the many corner shops in the district, in the days before cash and carry warehouses. Next to him is the 'one and only' wet fish shop, its marble slabs awash with water and bits of ice. Long, hanging rows of yellowy smoked haddock and brown kippers gaze down on generous cutlets of conger eel and slabs of salted cod, cheek by jowl with herrings and bloaters: enough to suit everyone's pocket and tastes. Outside this shop, an unusual stall exhibits rolls of the new American cloth, in various colours and designs. This 'gingham' oilcloth was sold by the yard for covering the wooden kitchen tables in everyday use and was, of course, washable. Narrow strips would be used as overmantel covers, the little shelf above the fireplace, and no doubt brightened the kitchen with their cheerful colours.

One of the busier shops comes next along the market, Batch's. Dozens of crates of eggs were laid open and the various sizes priced. These were imported from Poland and Denmark, nestled in wood shavings. Those that came cracked were sold in large trays at knock-down prices – 9d and 1s per dozen. There was a brisk trade in eggs sold loose in bags (no boxes or cartons in those days). Opposite the egg shop is one of the real characters of Chrisp Street market, Ernie Pike, the open-air butcher. With no shop, he can be heard calling out eminently affordable prices for joints, bacon, chops, beef, pork and lamb. Most shoppers know to wait until last thing on a Saturday night to buy a joint for Sunday dinner, knowing that 'Pikey' would never let you go away empty-handed if it meant less meat to store until Monday. Nearing the end of the market, you might be caught by an amazing Jewish pavement salesman from the Best Goldstein shop. He would invariably have 'your size' at a 'very special' price, the item had 'just arrived' (even if it had been in stock for months). He never went into the store himself, just called out that you were coming in – brilliant salesmanship.

Finally, there is Harris's, the market's only jeweller. Wedding rings, all shapes and sizes, are offered on velvet trays, together with a 'free gift' with every one purchased. Lines of Ingersoll watches with the latest luminous dials, a must to see in the dark. Harris was not a pawnbroker, though; that was Thompson, whose side door was open all day for customers requiring discretion. On Monday morning, the long line of pledgers, most of them regulars, would have something with which to pay the rent man, the coal merchant and the grocer, to keep their family alive, if not exactly well fed until payday. That is, if they could keep themselves from entering one of the six, very busy public houses found within a half-mile in the market, and as many more in the streets behind.

ST LEONARD'S ROAD

Leading off the East India Dock Road, St Leonard's Road provided the residents of Poplar with more shops of every description. Starting on one side was the Commercial Gas Company, which occupied the long corner premises next to the family butchers, Mace, with its wonderful display of joints and a long rail of sausages. Raggett's, the newsagents, was one of the busiest shops in the district, hosts of delivery boys being dispatched with the morning, midday, mid-afternoon and evening editions. These had to be out on time. The next-door shop was the immaculate Maypole, wonderful stamped designs impressed in the large blocks of yellow butter ranged on the marble counter. Your purchases did not come from these, but were cut at the back, shaped in small blocks and deftly placed on the counter by the assistant, armed with two paddles of wood which made wavy lines in the butter, which was then handed to you, wrapped in greaseproof paper.

Mrs Nunn was the florist and made the best floral tributes your neighbours could buy. Anderson's, the wet fish shop, was manned by a cheerful crew of blue-aproned staff. Water was always left running over the fish – they weigh more when wet. Gates the tobacconist was a compact little shop that specialised in loose tobacco weighed on brass scales. If you asked him to, he would tip the tobacco straight into your pouch. Opposite Glasson's the furniture store was Billy Wells, the catmeat man. His little shop was just a housefront, his sitting room filled with chunks of horsemeat, waiting to be sliced and chopped into small pieces. These were sold on skewers from a large basket as Billy toured the district, calling 'Cat meat!' If his knock went unanswered, the skewers would be left under the doorknocker, out of reach of all but the most agile cats.

The double-fronted Stevens's provisions was one of the friendlier family shops in the neighbourhood. Next door was another children's delight, a sweetshop, with especially low-built counters to enable the smaller ones to see and ponder their purchases for a while. They also sold twopenny 'monster' bottles of pop, that would be shared by two or three children. A large greengrocer and fruiterer, Hall's took up three or four premises, boxes of fruit and veg coming and going at all hours. Mr Drake was the local street bookie, and he took advantage of the bustle around Hall's to ply his trade. Street bookmaking was illegal, but Drake's odds were never any better than those offered by Mr Ross, who operated just down the street.

Haines, the fried fish shop, always had a long line waiting to be served. Frying times would be announced on a board, and a penny bag of crackling – loose pieces of batter – was welcome when they cleaned out the large fish fryers. Perpetually crouched over his 'hobbying foot' sat Gallard, the local boot and shoe repairer, his mouth filled with tacks. The little woodshop, Paul's, had racks of timber, boards and beading of every description. Cornelius, an old shop, sold pungent hay, wheat and fodder, plus all the feed mixes for fowl, rabbits, pigeons and pets. English, the drapery and furniture shop, was a boon to many families, offering credit by weekly payments in advance.

Just behind St Leonard's Road was Culshaw's dairy and shop. Children of shopping mothers liked to visit the immaculately clean herd of cows in the yard, which could sometimes be seen grazing in the local parks. Pchedborski, a name to be conjured with, was another favourite of local children, who watched him slicing and bagging bread – so different from the loaves wrapped in flimsy white paper you would get at the baker's. Wimhurst, the Rolls-Royce of confectioners and ice cream makers, provided gorgeous sundaes in thick, conical tumblers with red cordial dispensed on the top. Another Anderson fish shop dabbled in wet fish, with the occasional fry-up; Yeo, the piano shop, displayed a good range of polished wooden instruments with weekly instalments offered to tempt the burgeoning middle classes.

St Leonard's Road.

With money in short supply, imaginative arrangements were needed, and Rawlinson's the drapery ran a pay-as-you-wear scheme through local clubs. A double-sized shop, five or six assistants were always on call. Opposite was the solemn, double-fronted shop of Adams, undertakers. The management dealt sympathetically and with dignity with local folk at times of bereavement and were well-recommended; a window display offered a number of styles of inscribed headstones. More lively, if not exactly a 'barbershop quartet' – they were too busy clipping, shaving and nattering to sing – were the stylists at Sargent's, the local barber. Looker's, the ironmongers, was an Aladdin's cave of oddities. If you could describe it, the assistants would find whatever you wanted; within minutes, a 'thingummy that goes round like that and stands up at the back' would be wrapped and your money taken. Reeves the stationers was much patronised for writing materials; notebooks, pens, pencils, blotting paper, bottles of ink in every colour and size. This was long before the ubiquitous Biro and the felt-tip pens of nowadays, and was a haven for students. A chemist's shop and its next-door neighbour, an electrical retailer, concluded a shopping 'precinct' that had just about something for everyone.

4

The General Strike, Pubs &
Street Traders

As a nine-year-old schoolboy, I witnessed one of the most momentous events of East End history, the General Strike of 1926, which I recall so clearly three quarters of a century later. I lived within yards of the East India Dock Road, the main arterial road serving all of London's sprawling docklands. Names such as East India, West India, Millwall, Surrey, Commercial, King George and Albert Docks have passed into legend or are inscribed on brave new housing developments. It was here that the strike began, fuelled by the anger and resentment of the working class people of Poplar and its neighbouring boroughs, and of the British miners and railwaymen's unions, on 3 May. Pickets were placed on the docks in round-the-clock shifts, ensuring that no goods were dispatched from the dockside or unloaded from ships. Hospitals, schools and prisons were the only destinations to which goods were allowed to be delivered, supervised by a small army of men with armbands who barricaded the gates. From time to time, mounted police and, eventually, troops with armoured cars would emerge to escort convoys of essential goods through the shouting pickets.

The children were sent to school every day and so kept out of the way; after school, however, my brother and I ran errands for neighbours seeking news, as there were no newspapers or radio for a time. We lived about thirty yards from Poplar police station. Patrols would be inspected by the Sergeant in the yard at the back, where normally stray dogs destined for Battersea Dogs' Home would be rounded up. Most of the policemen had relatives or neighbours among the pickets; theirs was a difficult job. They would be sent in to mop up behind the mounted squads from nearby Limehouse, who had quickly developed a reputation for putting down potential riots. The vast acreage of the docklands and travelling time between the docks and stables made it virtually impossible for so few police to control the situation. After they had left to change shifts and feed the horses, it was business as usual for the crowd. But there were few arrests; our local force could not afford to spend time writing reports and attending court for so little outcome.

Our local MP was George Lansbury, Independent Labour, who edited a workers' paper. Unable to publish his broadsheet, he set up a printing press at his home

Soldiers on their way to the Royal Albert and King George Docks during the General Strike, May 1926. A contingent had already been detached at the East India Dock by the time this was taken.

in Bow Road and issued a daily bulletin to keep the strikers informed. One issue advised strikers and pickets to wear their war medals when confronting the police or soldiers, to remind them that they had also fought 'for King and Country'. When the government brought in emergency powers, hundreds of special constables were recruited. Armed with long batons and striped police armbands, these 'specials' were not deployed in the East End, as few, probably, would have survived. The mob hated these 'blacklegs', as the strikebreakers were called. Some of the powers entrusted to the police were not made public, one being that if only two or three people were seen talking together, they could be told to break up and go home and arrested if they did not. This type of restriction caused a lot of hostility. My family and I witnessed some acts of brutality from our sitting room window; one man was pursued down the street by a policeman on horseback, who was striking him about the head with a baton. The neighbours all shouted to the policeman to leave him alone; the man, they knew, worked late at the hospital and was merely on his way home.

Right: Using armoured vehicles, strikebreakers moved food in convoy from the docks to the City during the General Strike of May 1926. In the background the Pavilion cinema is being extended to cope with the new fad for 'talking pictures'.

Below: Strikers stop a vehicle in Cotton Street at the back of the Poplar Pavilion where a film called The Iron Horse *was showing. A single mounted policeman tries to keep order.*

The Poplar rates dispute has become a forgotten bywater of history, but the numbers of protestors marching with banners to the High Court show that it was an all-too-real event for many people too poor to afford food in 1921.

Looking back now, I am astonished at the great division that the government created within the population at the time, a real sense of 'Us' and 'Them'. Within three years of the Armistice of 1918 there was severe poverty among miners and the families of thousands of unemployed servicemen who had fought for a better country to live in. The Labour party was ineffectual in those days and easily branded as Trotskyists and troublemakers, especially in the wake of the Russian revolution and the murder of the Tsar and his family, news of which had taken a long time to come out and was still fresh in the minds of the better-off classes. Poplar knew real poverty – at one time, all the elected members of Poplar Borough Council were put in prison for spending rate money on feeding the poor. To save face, the Government told the council to treat the money as a loan, which was never repaid. The means the Government used to put down the strike in 1926 were notorious; university 'freshers', polo-playing cavalrymen, Lords and Ladies drove lorries and organised rest stations and food kitchens for the well-to-do volunteers, who were going to 'show the dirty strikers' who was boss. The thousands of strikebreakers running the buses and the railways or joining the police were oblivious to the plight of the miners and

Women councillors address the crowd from the balcony of the town hall in Newby Place, 1921. Protest mounted after the Government had the members of Poplar Council arrested for diverting rates money to a voucher scheme to feed the starving during the Depression. After six weeks of demonstrations the councillors were freed.

their families in Yorkshire and Durham who were, literally, starving. Yet, such was the miners' spirit that they stayed locked-out for six months without even the meagre pay to which they might have been entitled.

The four main railway companies were the GWR, LNER, LMS and Southern. They recruited volunteers who, after one day's instruction, drove trains and operated signalboxes. There were casualties and breakdowns and a collision at Bishop's Stortford that cost one man his life. Outside Newcastle, strikers removed a section of track and derailed the famous engine, the *Flying Scotsman*. A navy submarine was brought up the Thames so that its generator could power an important food refrigeration plant after the Battersea Power Station shut down. Warships were dispatched to docks around the country and naval ratings coerced into unloading and turning-round cargo ships that had been unable to berth at London. Half the time, the Trades Union Congress and its General Strike Council had no idea of the draconian measures being taken by the government, which was determined to prevent the 'Revolution' breaking out in Britain.

The dependence of Poplar on coal for its industry and home heating reflected that of the country as a whole. The miners' strike was basically in the deep mines; coal seams close to the surface were now opened up and opencast mines appeared everywhere. Some of this low-grade fuel was dangerous, causing red-hot stones to fly out of the hearth and set fire to clothes and furnishings within range. Large dumps of this brown coal were set up and people encouraged to come and collect it for themselves. Boxes on wheels and even prams were used to cart the sacks away. A few enterprising deliverymen undercut the regular coalmen and sold half-hundredweight sacks of 'nutty slack' – mostly stones, dust and a lot of water if mined when wet. We never discovered if any of this fuel found its way into our local gasworks; we never seemed to run out of gas – anyway, our meter was always full of pennies. We could still buy coke – coal discarded from the retort houses after the gas had been extracted. But it was well into the following year of 1927 before we saw the return of the coalmen to our streets, with the best quality coal.

In its way, the General Strike, which lasted only nine days, showed the world that the working population of the UK had shown solidarity with the very poorest, despite government provocation, strikebreaking and harsh measures. During the six months' 'lockout' that followed, working-class organisations in Poplar and elsewhere provided much financial and practical support to Britain's miners, who as I write are now almost a vanished species.

DOWN THE PUB

Looking back through some old records I discovered sixty-one pubs in the Poplar area, including Limehouse and Millwall. These all bear the E14 district code, and many of them are described in this chapter, together with the names of the licensees and managers. They are, of course, all linked with various brewers, many of whose names survive, even if their owners have long departed. Watney, Coombe and Read; Truman Hanbury and Buxton; Mann Crossman and Pauline; Taylor Walker; Charrington's, Ind Coope; Lovibonds. The latter, possibly the least familiar now, seems to have served the many off-licences dotted about the local streets. On delivery days the draymen, in their leather aprons, would lower the full barrels and pull up the empty ones on ropes, lowered into the cellars via the pavement-level doors, often spilling beer dregs over the pavement. They were jolly, tubby chaps, fond of a laugh and a joke with the passers-by, who either had to step over, or go round the ropes to get by. The delivery note was taken into the bar to be signed, and as a reward for their hard work, a couple of pints would be set up on the bar. After a number of deliveries, it must be said, the horses needed to know their way home at the end of the day.

Bottled beer started a trend and Worthington's, Bass, India Pale and Newcastle Brown ales and, of course, Guinness, became a convenient way to go to the pub and get a few beers for your friends and family at home. To make an evening out on Saturday or Sunday, you dressed up. If you had cash in hand, you might stand a pal a drink if he was at the bar. Port and lemon was considered the ladies' drink and not too likely to lead them into trouble. Pubs often had a pianist and a singalong helped to make a good evening. Local talent was most popular, and a familiar ballad played and

The Aberfeldy Tavern, c. 1941. Some air raid damage can be seen at the corner of East India Dock Road and Aberfeldy Street, to where the pub eventually moved in 1946.

The Young Prince in Chrisp Street, on the corner of Southill Street, 1938. The happy regulars are assembled on the spot where the women sold clothes cheaply from a big heap piled on the road, and are awaiting the arrival of the charabanc to take them on an outing. Accordions were becoming increasingly popular.

The Resolute pub, Poplar High Street, 1936. The pub was rebuilt not long afterwards. One of the famous three-wheeled milk carts can be seen outside Hitchman's Dairy on the right.

sung with feeling would earn the virtuoso a pint from an appreciative member of the audience. Equally, it might result in a dousing in beer dregs for the player or the piano, from some likely lad who thought he was a laugh a minute.

Jug and bottle bars, sometimes known as off-licences because you could not drink on the premises, did a steady midweek trade. There was no enforcement of any age limit when I fetched a jug of beer for my nan or grandad. Usually the money was handed over along with an empty bottle, there being useful 'money-back' on the returns. In the days before they started putting nuts out on the bar, there were small bowls of very salty shrimps; the salt was to encourage your thirst. For the children outside, peering in at the door, pubs sold biscuits, usually arrowroot, dry and tasteless. Later, along came the famous Smith's Crisps, each bag containing a measure of salt screwed up in blue greaseproof paper. Nevertheless, the salt was always wet and it took a hard shake to get it all evenly distributed. Little packets of four biscuits interlaid with strong soft cheese were another favourite, made by Meredith & Drew. They cost twice as much as the arrowroot ones. The thick glasses beer was served in usually bore the name of the pub, but this small precaution did not stop the stock from diminishing,

The St Leonard's Arms stood immediately opposite St Michael and All Angels' Church. Dewberry Street is on the left, and Mercer was the publican from 1934 until 1952. The actor Terence Stamp mentions it in his autobiography, Stamp Album, *as being a regular haunt of his grandmother.*

The Volunteer, East India Dock Road. By the time this was taken in the 1960s much of the life of Poplar had gone, including the Grand Picture Palace and Karamel's sweetshop. The pub itself was eventually demolished in the early 1990s.

The White Horse, Poplar High Street, 1926. The façade dates from about 1868 and the pub was rebuilt in 1929, to vanish completely in 2001. A tavern is believed to have stood on the site since the late 1600s and a very much older building houses Whale's Ice Cream Powders to the right. On the far right can be seen a corner of the shop owned by a Chinese family who ran a 'Puk-a-poo', an illegal betting den.

especially if the beer was taken to be drunk outside when there was someone you did not wish to meet at the bar.

The darts contest between the pubs in the locality was a moneyspinner for publicans. Some matches between invited teams went on well after closing time. The lights would go out around the bar, doors locked; they were officially and indisputably 'closed'. No beer was supposed to be served after the bell went for 'Time!', and the last few rounds of the match would be played in subdued silence, rather than risk a visit from the Law. Winners and losers would be let out of the side door, a few at a time, to avoid causing a disturbance. Today's jukeboxes and video games would have been a turn-off for the hardened drinkers of those days. But some piano-less pubs welcomed door buskers, who came round mostly in pairs. One would go in with a cap to catch a few pennies, while the other would keep a foot in the door and start singing, whistling or playing the spoons or bones. Though not all were appreciated, some of the singers had good voices. Young ladies, wives and occasionally a teenager would give a rendering of a popular song, sometimes in an Irish or Welsh accent.

Among the regular callers were the Salvation Army girls, the 'Sally Ann', who came in while the band played in the street outside. Selling a few copies of *War Cry* with a sweet smile usually brought them a few coins, sometimes a 'bob' (shilling) from the landlord; the paper was mostly left unread. When a full band was not available, an officer would play on a small, portable harmonium, accompanied by a few girls on tambourines. Setting up halfway between two pubs was most efficient.

Other pubs in Poplar were the weekly meeting-places of the working men's fellowship societies, the Buffaloes, Oddfellows, the Loan Club and the HSA night. For these a room or bar was generally set aside. When I was running one such night I had to collect sixpence a week from each member, which insured their family against the cost of hospital treatment. The fishing clubs, and the pigeon fanciers all had their nights, as did the rowers in the pubs nearer the river. Sometimes clubs would contribute to Christmas funds for the children, to pay for a party, perhaps with a conjuror.

Temporary bar staff were always a problem in the days before the 'upside-down' optic dispensers and glasses with an official 'plimsoll line' came into

The Bromley Hall Tavern, Brunswick Road, Bromley, with Zetland Street on the right. Built in 1902, the pub was demolished in 1971 to make way for the widening of the northern approach road to the Blackwall Tunnel. The Baptist Tabernacle stood on the opposite corner.

The Railway Tavern, West India Dock Road with, inset, landlord Charlie Brown. The uncrowned 'King of Limehouse', Charlie was a genuine East End legend, turning his pub into a museum with an astonishing collection of priceless Ming vases, Sèvres cabinets and other curios. The King of Spain once visited the pub incognito (introducing himself as 'Alf') to inspect the trophies, which took him two hours. Hugely wealthy, Charlie was a tireless worker on behalf of hundreds of charities. When he died in 1932 at the age of seventy-three, work in the docks stopped for his funeral and police had to force a way through the crowds who lined Burdett Road to Bow cemetery five deep.

use. Arguments frequently resulted from customers sensing short measure, especially when bought with a 'mixer' such as tonic or Vermouth. Another serious complaint was when the barman, on being offered a drink, would show a half-full glass and be happy to 'have one later'. He would then put the money by the till and pocket it after the customer had gone. Tipsy customers, too, seldom queried their change, providing opportunities for sharp barmen.

As well as the landlord and his wife or whole family helping to run a well-organised pub, they could not do without the man they called the 'potman'. He fulfilled many duties, including collecting up the empty glasses for washing from around the pub, outside and along the surrounding streets, yards and gardens. He always managed to find five or six that were not quite empty and would sup these on the way back. He also helped to bring up crates from the cellar at busy times. A good potman would always ask politely if a customer's glass was empty before lifting it. A considerate, well-dressed potman was an asset to a pub and, if trusted, the landlord kept him on in regular employment and he never had to pay for his drink; like the drayman's horse, he always found his way home.

STREET TRADERS

Mostly they would come to the front door, preceded by their cries, at regular times and on set days. Often the purchase would be only a penny or two, but they were always grateful for the regular custom and left with a cheery word before resuming their hawker's cry. Retailing was more specialised then, a personal business. For the womenfolk tied to the home by endless chores, cleaning and cooking for the family, or caring for elderly relatives, their visits were a welcome break from the daily drudgery. They were the street vendors, or hawkers; now mostly vanished characters from the East London stage.

The Coal Man

Coal was delivered on carts in half-hundredweight sacks of 'nuts' or 'best': nuts for the kitchens, best in larger lumps for the open grates. London's world-famous 'fog' of course arose from the sulphur smoke of thousands upon thousands of coal-burning chimneys: there was no central heating! When delivered, you immediately broke up the larger pieces for burning. The impact of the hammer scattered tiny fragments

The staff of Cade's coal depot, c. 1930. Joseph Cade & Co. were the reputable coal merchants in Longnor Road, Mile End. They successfully saw off competition during the Depression years from 'freelance' operators selling inferior coal.

everywhere. These were shovelled up for banking the hot embers. Kings of the local coal merchants were Coe, Wilson and Grover. Regulars frequently had to see off, or put up with, less reputable freelance operators.

The Milkmen

With their noisy, rattling cans hooked to the sides of their curious barrows, the milkmen did not need to call out as they made their way along the potholed streets. You got plenty of notice to fetch your empty can and replenish it from the big churn. Pushing and steering the three-wheeled barrows was an acquired skill; the front wheel was the turning axis and to negotiate a corner or an obstacle required a lot of strength. Hitchman's from Kirby Street had the largest rounds; supplies were obtained direct from Culshaw's dairy, where the cows stood, unnaturally clean in the spotless, whitewashed yard.

The Muffin Man

Yes, they really existed! This character of story and rhyme was for some reason seen and heard, mainly on dark winter or cold late autumn evenings. The clanging of his brass bell and his call as he waited at the street corner could be heard over a wide neighbourhood of households. His tray of muffins, dough buns covered in a nice, green felt, was balanced on his head. Customers would wait until the tray was lifted down and a stick put under it, to act as a leg. The muffins themselves would still be familiar today: you can buy them in supermarkets.

The Shrimp and Winkle Seller

This trader usually called around the streets on Sunday mornings. He never seemed to come later than 12.30, giving the impression that his produce was caught fresh with the morning tide. You would buy the shellfish, sometimes with a stick of celery or a bunch of watercress, which he sold separately, for tea. Whelks and mussels, too, were spread out on a large, white sheet on the floor of his horse-drawn cart. Your purchases would be ladled into a brown paper bag for weighing. He always called out 'Gravesend shrimps!' as you left. It was his calling card.

The Toffee Apple Man

Summer brought the toffee apple man, pushing a small, wooden box on wheels between two long shafts. The toffee apples were carefully laid out in rows, their sticks all pointing straight up. Toffee running down the apples would puddle on the bottom, leaving a squashed blob known as a 'flat'. We searched for the biggest 'flats' we could find. Sometimes, the toffee apple man sold 'flats' by themselves, if he had run out of the soft eating apples; or he might just hand one to you. It was a job to keep the smaller apples on the stick after the first bite. The toffee stuck to your teeth and lips and even your nose, if you were too anxious to get to the middle.

The Grinders

Knife and scissors grinders were rarely seen in our street as so many people ground their own knives on the broken paving slabs they somehow acquired. When one did appear, my mother would get a price for sharpening the scissors, as father could never manage to get a good edge on those. The grinder would sit on his seat and operate a treadle attached by a leather belt to the spindle in the centre of the grinding wheel. Now and then, he would pour a little water over the stone from a small can that swung under the barrow. Sparks flew, then a wipe with a rag and the article would be brought to the door, where the keenness of the edge would be demonstrated on a thick pad of newsprint.

Rag and Bone Men

In later years these became general scrap dealers; however, their original stock in trade was old clothing and animal bones, which had a variety of uses. Nothing was wasted; recycling is not a modern invention. At the familiar cry you looked to see who

This team of coopers, photographed in the 1930s, worked for John William Sayers of Ropery Street, Bow. The firm was kept busy between its foundation in 1881 and 1957, making and repairing beer barrels for all the breweries in the neighbourhood.

it was, as several of the street hawkers gave good prices. In our street they were on to a loser, however, as we had a resident shop, Hyman's, where most of our rags and bones went, although my mother always complained of being short-changed. Now and then a barrow man would present you with a windmill, gaily fluttering in the wind, instead of cash; a skipping rope, or even a live newt or goldfish.

Door Knocker Painters

This 'little man' had few tools to carry: two small tins on a wooden frame, one holding brushes, the other black lead paint, which he was continually having to stir. Most people in those poor neighbourhoods took a fierce pride in their front doors and steps, the women on their hands and knees, whitewashing the grimy stonework and a half-circle of pavement around. Woe betide anyone who walked on the newly painted pavement! The door knocker painter would attach a card to the door, warning of wet paint for the next 24 hours. At Number 20 we had a brass letterbox, which was properly polished every week by my dad.

The Ice Cream Man

The first ice cream man who ever came to our street was an Italian. Despite his rudimentary grasp of English he knew how many pennies made a shilling. His ice cream was a solid vanilla block wrapped in what looked like blotting paper, sold from a barrow. The call then was 'Assenheim's', this being the not-very catchy brand sold at the time. It soon went out of fashion, to be replaced by Wall's. The little three-wheeled carts had the famous slogan: 'Stop me and buy one!'. Ices, vanilla blocks and tubs came out of cold boxes that steamed when the lid was lifted. A man with a horse and cart occasionally came and people would bring out their own containers for him to scoop the ice cream into from a block, topped off with a wafer.

Posy Sellers

On weekend evenings at the height of summer, two or three young ladies would appear in the High Street, between twelve and fifteen years of age. They were selling small bud roses wrapped in silver paper and finished off with a fine sprig of fern. The roses gave off a lovely perfume. They were kept fresh with a sprinkle of water from a lemonade bottle tucked away in a basket on the pavement. Girlfriends would accept these small tokens gladly and, now and then, the lads would sport them in their buttonholes.

Chimneysweeps

The chimneysweeps did a good trade in Poplar, the brush being the only method they used in the 1920s and '30s. The brush had to appear out of the top of the chimney pot and one of the family had to go outside to make sure it had come out. On dry days, the soot flew everywhere in the house, and piles of ground salt would be kept ready – this made it easier to sweep up the soot. In addition to the many fires caused

Not just a humble chimneysweep, Thomas Brooks was Mayor of Bethnal Green in 1931/2 and a Councillor for thirty-four years. He began sweeping chimneys at the age of twelve, and it was said of his election to mayor that he was 'well sooted' to the task. (© Hulton-Getty Collection)

by burning tarry blocks and impure coal, which caused the soot to build up rapidly inside the flue, chimneys would be deliberately set alight to save the cost of a sweep. They would be hurriedly put out by the guilty occupant, hopefully before a neighbour raised the alarm and the fire brigade appeared.

Dockyard Tea 'Boys'
Near the docks, it was a regular sight to see a man carrying a stick, about three feet long. This had nails sticking out and six or seven mugs swinging from them, filled with steaming tea from the local café. The café did a very good trade with the dockers and usually stopped serving when the tea boy appeared. There was quite a distance to walk back to the dockside with the mugs of tea, carrying any other purchases the men had requested. Dock tea runs started at 7.30 in the morning and went on until 10.00. One tea boy told me he had never done any dock work: he had been taken on for this job alone. I never saw them work in the afternoons.

Pub Buskers

We lived next-door-but-one to a public house and, as there was virtually no other sound in our living room apart from conversation and the occasional argument, we could hear clearly the noises coming from there. In the quiet of the night we would hear singing, and know that the saloon bar door had been rudely pushed open by a pair of buskers. One kept his boot in the door while the other gave a rendering of a popular song of the day, before passing the hat. Then, we might hear the sound of a pair of spoons being hammered, back to back, up and down the player's body to accompany the singing, which varied in quality. 'Martha', 'Danny Boy' and 'Ramona, I hear the mission bells above' were the usual fare. Some nights more than one pair of buskers would come along, much to the annoyance of the publican.

Street Buskers

There were many entertainers in the streets. Some would hire a barrel organ and push it all the way to Poplar. The operator would keep cranking the handle, and the barrel organ would play three or four songs while a colleague passed the hat around, collecting from passers-by. Sometimes a third man would tap-dance or sing, dressed as a woman, in a high-pitched voice to amuse the children. Other organ grinders kept a monkey on a chain that would dance or cleverly hold out the hat for people to toss coins into. Sometimes there would be a duet, with a trumpet and piano-accordion. These were becoming the vogue, replacing the old concertina, which was associated with out-of-work seamen and the Salvation Army. There were solo singers, too, the men loud and deep-throated, turning their heads from side to side to let the sound radiate far down the streets around. Arthur Tracy, the famous street singer, copied this technique for the music halls he performed in.

The Side Street 'Unofficial' Traders

They stood at the top of a street where it joined the market, keeping a wary eye out for the market inspectors, ready to move on hurriedly at the sight of a peaked cap. Regular shady traders were the silk stocking men who worked from a battered suitcase down by their feet. Their cry as they held up a perfect stocking with their hand inside was 'Every pair bears inspection!' but it sometimes didn't, when you opened up the bag hopefully containing the colour you had asked for. You might have a pair that did not match, or that was laddered before the lady even put them on. By the time you returned, the silk stocking man would be long gone, perhaps to the next market if he had lots of goods to shift.

The Round Elastic Man

This highly specialised salesman was another 'unofficial' trader. He wandered up and down the market crying 'Best round elastic!' Actually what he sold was not round at all but more like tape, white and in various widths. Where it went was 'round' the leg or waist! Quite a lot of elastic was used by the poor people in those days, for socks, knickers and tied under the chin to keep a child's hat or bonnet on, to mention only a few uses. The elastic was sold by the foot or yard and measured with the 18-inch rule he kept hidden inside his coat.

The Horseradish and Mint Man

My dear friend George White was the mainstay of his family, one of the nicest and most hardworking men I ever had the pleasure of meeting. They were very poor, his mother was widowed, and George kept an allotment near the railway station, where he grew horseradishes and bushes of mint. He ground up the horseradish roots on a little board that hung from a string round his neck, packing the portions into little white bags. An essential accompaniment to the Roast Beef of Old England, his horseradish was sold by him from a pitch as near as he could get to the butcher's. When the season arrived for spring lamb, he sold sprigs of mint to make mint sauce. Rain or shine, he was always there, sometimes drenched, and he would help any trader in the market, especially if a few extra shillings could come his way after his stock had sold out.

The Razor Blade Seller

After safety razors arrived, you bought replacement blades in packets of five, wrapped in greaseproof paper. Gillette, Seven o'Clock and Ever Ready were the most popular brands. The razor blade seller was another 'unofficial' trader who did not need to rent a stall, as a cardboard box held in his hand contained six packets of blades. He would stand as far away as possible from the chemist or the barber's shop, and his prices were coppers below those regular suppliers, with their overheads. Where his supplies came from, nobody knew. Suspicions grew, however, when he 'could not get any more' at the price he had been offering!

The Salt Seller

This chap had such a small barrow, it would have been a crime for the market inspectors to have charged him anything for a pitch. Strategically positioned near my friend the pot herb lady, in case of shoppers planning a stew, he had a block of salt perched on a cart with four small pram wheels, to which was attached a rusty saw. His cry was: 'Don't forget your salt, ma', an idea later borrowed by the advertising agency for Rowntrees Fruit Gums. He would saw off a portion and wrap it in a piece of newsprint; two if it was raining. My mother gave us boys the job of pulverising the blocks of salt into a jam jar, with a finer grinding for the salt cellar on the table, whose tiny spoon was always getting lost.

The Lamplighter

When we played on the streets as children, even after dark, no one thought of us as being in danger from child molesters or hit-and-run drivers. Often a door would open and a parent would call out, but the sound of shouting and laughter reassured them you were out there somewhere. As it got darker, up would come the lamplighter on his bike, steering with one hand as he balanced with the other, the long ignition pole which he carried on his shoulder. The top of the pole engaged with a lever on the lamp standard and opened the gas valve; a lighted wick completed the job, bathing the dark streets in pools of wan light so that we could play outside for a few hours longer. I often watched him light the lamps, but I never saw him turn them off – I was still fast asleep.

The Cat Meat Man

I have mentioned him earlier. He was very popular and had a shop in St Leonard's Road and a long round throughout Poplar. He carried a very large basket, inside were the cut-up cubes of (mostly) horsemeat and a bundle of sharp-pointed skewers, which he would thrust through a dozen or so pieces of meat at a time, calling out 'Cat meat!'. If there was nobody in, he would leave the skewers under the door knocker, out of reach of the interested neighbourhood cats. It might remain there for several hours before anyone came home. I never saw him wearing a tie or scarf, just a narrow, white collar, stained with grease.

The Indian Sweet Man

When this gentleman first appeared on our streets he was viewed with a certain amount of trepidation. But he was always polite and smiling and, of course, he was especially nice to us younger customers, who would nervously hang back before handing over our coppers, to receive the twirled-up spun sugar on a stick that all children today would recognise as candy-floss. To contain this mountain of joy he had a tin box, about three feet square, slung around his shoulder on a wide leather strap. After serving the children he would move on a few yards, tinkling a little brass bell. He would leave us flapping away at the wasps that swarmed in summer, attracted by the sugary smell. Strangely, they never seemed to go after the Indian sweet man.

The Newsboys

Young lads who could not find work on leaving school often became newsboys. Not the usual ones you imagine, getting up early in the morning to deliver papers and magazines on their rounds, these older lads were in a class of their own. At about eleven each morning they would start out from the paper shop with a big bundle under their arms, calling out 'Mid-day!' or 'Classified!' as they dashed about. The only time they stopped briefly was when someone wanted to buy a paper. Their second round was between five and six in the evening, when the cries changed to 'Final!' 'All the results!' and 'Prices', advertising the editions containing the afternoon's racing results, and the closing prices on the London Stock Exchange for the homegoing City workers.

The horse vet, seen in his surgery doorway at 773 Commercial Road, Limehouse, with his tough-looking assistants. The job often involved putting down horses injured in traffic accidents. He would regularly attend on horseback as it was quicker than using the lorry.

The Horse Vet

I spent all my young days watching horses and carts of all kinds, laden and unladen, passing by our house. You sometimes came across the horrible scene of a horse having to be put out of its misery. One bolted straight through a large glass shopfront and severely injured itself. People tried to help the poor driver free the horse from its twisted reins and harness, and covered it with sacks and mats. When the vet rode up on horseback, after what seemed like hours, he put a gun to its head and shot it. The crowd drifted away, and neighbours came with buckets of hot water and carbolic to wash down the pavement. The horse was carted away meanwhile to the slaughterhouse, to be turned into cat meat, no doubt. Such incidents stay in your memory.

The Blacksmith

There were two local smiths who were often called away from their anvils and forges to attend to a horse with a lost or bent shoe. Drivers cared for their animals, mostly, they were their livelihood, and they would not want to move without the horse being properly shod, so the smithy would have to go to them. Sometimes, their skills, brawn and tools would be needed for other jobs: iron bending, straightening or hammering home some part that had become attached or detached from a vehicle. Sometimes the vehicle had to be lifted up while they got underneath. I was fascinated by these 'men of steel', either in their yards or in our streets.

Glaziers

We had two of these tradesmen, riding along the street on their three-wheeled bikes with a wooden box slung on the back. Small sheets of glass were carefully wrapped in felt, and the boxes packed with tins of putty, tacks and nails and, of course, a small hammer. A brush pan and bags to take away the broken glass completed their toolkit. They reminded me a lot of the Charlie Chaplin film where Jackie Coogan as the young lad was sent round the streets with his catapult to break the windows while the tramp, as his father, came along to mend them. Our men had no ladder, so they had to go inside the houses and sit on the windowsills to complete their work.

The Blind Match Seller

You may be old enough to remember these tragic survivors on the streets of London, but unless you are as old as I am, you will almost certainly have no impression of how terribly young they were in those early days. Usually in their twenties or early thirties, they would tap their way about, unless accompanied, or stand on the corner with a tray of matches, calling out 'Camp!' or 'Bryant & May's!', being the rival brands of matches. The white tray would contain about six boxes, with a space left for the poorer women shoppers, mostly, to leave a few coppers, their only income. Often, the matches were not needed or even taken. A card on the tray and perhaps a campaign medal would give a stark reminder of where their sight had been given for their country: Mons, Ypres, the Somme. Blind charities like St Dunstan's or Lord Roberts's Workshops were in their infancy, but did wonderful work in later years.

Hot Chestnuts

These two words bring back the inviting smells, and the warmth and friendliness of the hot chestnut sellers who stood vigil on cold nights from mid-September until the Christmas season. The nicer one stood at the top of Chrisp Street, on the daytime site of the Burgess fruit stall. He would do his best trade on weekend evenings, catching the passers-by in the East India Dock Road. Steadily stoking his well-stocked brazier of coke, chatting to the customers, the operation of cutting the nuts with a cross was performed with great dexterity, the nuts placed on the red-hot iron sheet to roast. Every now and then he would flip them to do the other side, then quickly shovel some for a customer off the top of the heap into a small, white paper bag. It was not only chestnuts; the back of the stove had a box containing six well-pricked potatoes, little puffs of steam signifying readiness. He would cut them for you, or hand you a drum of salt if you wanted to eat on the premises. As a small boy, I remember him making up hot cordial drinks from the kettle that always stood on the side of the chestnut griddle. There was a choice of blackcurrant, peppermint or sarsaparilla. We asked him hundreds of questions, this friendly little man, but he always knew the answers.

Street buskers collect their barrel organs from Faccini's Piano Hire warehouse in Ernest Street, Stepney, early 1920s.
(© Topham Picture Library)

French Onion Sellers

They came between the months of May and September, an invasion of Frenchmen on heavy, black Peugeot bicycles. They wore berets, and striped Breton shirts, and had long strings of large, juicy onions slung over their shoulder, of a size that, with Bulldog perversity, we called 'Spanish'. In point of fact, we had three greengrocers already in the street they patrolled, and within about 50 yards another six vegetable stalls in Chrisp Street market! All, I am sure, sold identical onions, probably cheaper. Sometimes you would see a conclave of three or four, all with those thin, Clark Gable moustaches. One young housewife near us would stand at the door and engage them in conversation, probably improving their English. An onion would be detached from a string, and the man would pedal away. They never called out, just stood on the corner looking around, hoping someone would accost them. I wonder where, really, they came from? Why? Who paid their fares? How many onions did they have to sell to make any money at all?

The local dust cart, ready to start work.

The Rope Mat Mender

Of the thousands of terraced houses in Poplar, few had carpets or lino in their passageways: just bare boards, or now and again a strip of oilcloth along those long, narrow confines. The family would enter straight from the street, bringing with them all the dust and grime, so very often, rope (nowadays known as coir) mats would be put down to trap the worst of it. These quickly became worn and frayed, and the mender man would come round and look up each passageway and point out those that would benefit from his big needle and tough string thread. A deal agreed, he would sit on your doorstep and quickly save you the cost of a new mat, often joining together pieces of those that were otherwise past repairing. The things our mums had to do to save money!

Dustmen

The poor horse pulling the heavy, open dust cart was always surrounded by a swarm of flies. As the cart trundled by, the loose canvas flaps would be thrown aside, the battered, flimsy bins lifted from the kerbside and banged against the inside to empty them. If still about, the lids seldom fitted well after such treatment. We had to carry our dustbin, with the house number painted on it, all the way round from the backyard. With so little packaging, the rubbish consisted mainly of materials that could not be recycled: dust, ash and unburnable cinders from the kitchen and the scullery copper, which burned continuously, summer and winter. Nothing that could be used for fuel was thrown away. Even tea leaves were used to bank the fire in winter so that hot water and breakfast could be ready for the early workers. Our dustman was always polite and gave us a knock the week before Christmas. He was one of the few who received a Christmas box, as it used to be known.

The Vinegar Man

A dear old man who came to our turning every week, he was so tiny that I am sure even the poorest people of the streets felt sorry for him as he pushed his barrow along. On this was mounted a wooden barrel with a tap at the bottom, and below this hung a small Nestlé milk tin to catch the drips. You brought an empty, clear-glass lemonade bottle, with the screw stopper, and he would fill it, pouring a tankard measure through a funnel. You could see you were getting full measure. The strong malt vinegar seemed to have twice the flavour of that which you liberally sprinkled over your bag of chips at the fish shop. Their watered-down version stood next to the large salt shakers on the counter, to which you helped yourself liberally for free before the meal was wrapped in its white paper and taken home.

The Carbolic and Firewood Man

In the warm weather, when the gullies, drains and roads had no rainwater to flush them, this man did a roaring trade. The smells of the factories seemed to fill the air; the gutters were choked with dust, dog and horse droppings; backyard toilets developed a noxious odour. He would fill your R. White's or Western lemonade bottle straight from the barrel on his barrow, while publicans would bring a small container and douse their backyard public toilets liberally with the strong, white disinfectant, leaving white puddles lying around for days. To walk through them was to sanitise the soles of your boots for life. The bundles of chopped firewood, tied with tarred string, were brought into the house and carefully stacked on a shelf in the hallway, to be used only when absolutely necessary. The combined smells of carbolic and tar lingered for years.

Kate the Washerwoman

On a Monday morning Kate could be seen pushing a flat-top trolley like a big pram along the street, knocking at the doors of her regulars. She was only about four feet eight tall and sometimes was hardly visible above the pile of washing she had collected. This she took to the public baths, which were equipped with tubs, hot water and tables to lay out and check the items taken in for washing. There were wringers, too – but not enough: you could wait your turn, sometimes for quite a while. This caused hard feelings among the women, always pressed for time. Otherwise, they would exchange the news and gossip of the past week over the soapsuds and the washboards. I never found out how Kate knew what washing belonged to which customer, or what the rate of pay was for her services, but she was a great help to busy mothers and the ones who were expecting babies in particular came to rely on her a lot.

The Gas Meter Man

Once a month my mother's daily routine would be interrupted by news from along the street that the gasman was coming to empty the meter. I stood or sat on the passage floor and watched the ritual of the meter box being emptied on to the mat. The pennies were piled into stacks of twelve to a shilling, to make up five shillings, which would then be put in a blue coin bag and several of these, if the meter was full, went into one large Gladstone bag. The rebate was always welcome, I never knew my mum to question the amount: it was all written up in his book and then the meter man would move on to the next house in the street. Before closing time at 3.30 he had to deposit his heavy bag at the bank; anything he took later would accompany him home, to be banked in the morning. Saving gas was obligatory in our house, all our evening activities were concentrated around the one gas mantle, which made a good target for missiles and sometimes got broken, with many denials. We always went to bed by candlelight but later there was a gas bracket in the bedroom, with an eerie flame like a Bunsen burner, which the oldest boy was trusted to light.

The Gypsy Ladies

When I was a small boy, in my storybooks gypsy ladies sat around a fire with a cauldron suspended on three stakes, cooking a meal. It was a surprise then when four gypsy ladies wearing colourful headscarves alighted from the Number 65 tram clutching one small baby and several large baskets. Descending on Ida Street, where we lived, they split up, two to each side of the street, and began knocking. We were instructed to close the door if they were on the step as the washing was hung in the passageway and we did not trust them. Mother would take a copper or two – never her purse – and inspect the basket of wares. Skeins of black or grey darning wool, small packets of needles, cards of white linen, coated tin buttons of various sizes: twopence was usually enough to purchase something. If nothing took Mum's fancy, sprigs of 'lucky white heather' would be produced amid much wheedling. Mum never did succumb to their entreaties to cross their palms with silver and have her future told; she reckoned that had been settled when she married my father. Dad said the Gypsies parked their caravans on Wanstead Flats, where the men could be seen cutting wood to make clothes pegs.

The Mussel Man

A big man wearing a blue fisherman's jersey summer and winter used to stand on the corner of Grundy Street and call 'Mussels!' or sometimes 'Fresh Belgian mussels!'. He sold them by the quart pot, which would be emptied into a strong brown paper bag. The mussels, which were imported daily from Ostend, were still wet from his bucket. This gave them a fresh, shiny appearance while he toured the streets. We only tried them once when my new brother-in-law Arthur, who was a Poplar policeman, brought home a big bag and cooked them himself for his tea, much to the disgust of my sister. I think he had acquired a taste for them while serving in Belgium during the First World War – more likely than in Dulwich, where he was born and brought up.

The Travelling Roundabout Man

The clanging of a handbell brought the youngest children rushing in excitement to their doors. Outside was a horse and cart with a red, white and blue painted roundabout, revolving slowly. This was worked by the man turning a large handwheel beneath the cart. On the cart was a box containing dozens of glass and stone jam jars. One jar was the 'fare' for a turn on the eight-seater roundabout, which creaked at every turn while the poor horse stood still, the cart kept stationary by means of a chain running through the spokes of the wheels. The mums and aunts stood by, ready to lift off the children when their turn ended. I wonder what that man did with all those jars, to earn a crust?

Silk Scarves and Gaudy Ties

Every spring a small stream of Indian gentlemen would issue from a disused shop in Grundy Street, each carring a small suitcase. Over their shoulders would be draped a motley selection of brightly coloured scarves and ties. Opened on your doorstep, should you show interest, the cases proved to be crammed with more gaudy neckware. These salesmen all seemed identical, their black hair shining with what looked like Brilliantine. In the evening they all returned to the shop, never hurrying, but walking with a sort of shuffle. In the late evening they would reappear in small groups and sit on the pavement, either getting fresh air or just waiting to go to bed. They had a manager in charge of the team, who allocated them an area, supplied the goods and deducted the money for board and lodgings. They were familiar with British money and never gave discounts.

The Baker's Boy

We always called him the baker's boy but in reality he was in his forties. He sometimes had a real boy with him, who would knock each side of the street to let the mothers know he had arrived. Inside the four-wheeled cart was a crowd of newly baked loaves: cottage loaves, split tins, bloomers, sandwich tins, small brown loaves and crusty rolls. Some of the rolls had been too long in the oven and were burned black. Underneath the cart was a long drawer concealing scones, doughnuts, jam tarts and both types of flour you could get then, plain and self-raising! Now and again, yesterday's loaves would be available cheaply to a good customer. They made a good bread pudding. The bakers used out-of-time bread themselves to produce what we called 'mince', small slabs of a bread pudding cake with sultanas and raisins, baked on the outside with a layer of flaky pastry, very filling. More so than the fairy cake sponges with a little piece of cherry stuck on top. Your penny had to go a long way to fill your stomach.

The Tally Men

No list of Poplar street characters would be complete without the tally men, those hardworking doorstep credit brokers. Two were very active in our area. One was Mr Anderson, who owned a shop in Abbots Road. He and his wife called round regularly on Fridays and Saturdays and collected cash from their customers.

The fair visits Poplar Recreation Ground, 1919.

Often, the smallest member of the family would open the door and announce that 'mother says she is out', and battle would commence. The other was a green young salesman from Blundell's in City Road. He booked orders and would take a small deposit, perhaps for a pair of blankets or some sheets and pillowcases. It was all on trust; suing for payment was nigh on impossible and too expensive. The large parcel would arrive from the well-known carriers, Carter Paterson, and would be signed for by 'John Bull', 'L. Kitchener' or 'W.G. Grace'. The carrier never queried the signature. The goods would then be unwrapped and taken next day to the pawnshop. Blundell's could never prove it had been delivered, as the grumbling householder would complain when the young man returned. They would demand a refund of their deposit, saying that they had changed their minds. The final outcome of these tricks would be that the pawn ticket was offered around the district at a reduced rate, to anyone who wanted a nice new pair of blankets or some bedlinen.

5

The Blitz

Many readers now in their sixties and older will bear witness to the events that occurred in the early days of the bombing of East London; the lucky escapes, the devastation, the tragedies – not forgetting the many heroic deeds that Poplar and East End people performed as wardens, heavy rescue, fire and ambulance service workers, or just as good neighbours. A number of their stories and pictures are to be found in *My East End*, by Anita Dobson. In my story, though, I have moved on years and advanced my position in the offices of Fraser and Fraser Ltd, whom I joined in 1937.

The early months of the war until the spring of 1940 were a time known as the Phoney War. Nothing much happened – but that did not stop us from mounting a large *Daily Express* battle map on a sheet of cardboard. Two sets of coloured pins were moved back and forth daily, after consulting newspapers and listening to the BBC news. Once we had to start again, after the office cleaners erased the battlefront by tidying up the pins. I was called up and required to attend a medical in Ilford, but graded C3, which kept me out of the services. Our works and office staff got fewer and it was becoming hard to find suitable replacements.

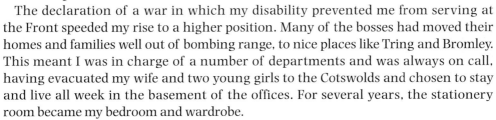

The declaration of a war in which my disability prevented me from serving at the Front speeded my rise to a higher position. Many of the bosses had moved their homes and families well out of bombing range, to nice places like Tring and Bromley. This meant I was in charge of a number of departments and was always on call, having evacuated my wife and two young girls to the Cotswolds and chosen to stay and live all week in the basement of the offices. For several years, the stationery room became my bedroom and wardrobe.

Our factory was situated alongside the District Line railway, and at the bottom of the yard was a wharf on the River Lea, from where we got our water supply. The railway line went over the river and then across the Regent's Canal. On the other side of the railway station, which was next to our building, was a large gasworks with two huge gasometers and next to this, on the other side of our building, was

St Andrew's Hospital. The road outside led to Bow Bridge and then on to the Blackwall Tunnel. Strategically speaking, my temporary home was smack bang in the middle of Bomber's Paradise, and the noise at times was very frightening. Somehow, I emerged unscathed.

The RAF ordered underground petrol storage tanks from us and dug holes all over the Home Counties to conceal them in. We also made decontamination tanks and equipment for the Ministry. As the demands of the war gathered momentum, orders were flooding in from the Drawing Office with lists of items required down to the smallest nut and bolt, and our stocks of steel were soon exhausted. Yet we had to replace it or lose business to our competitors – not everything had changed.

For the Army, we made dozens of armour-plated cabs to protect the drivers of troop carriers; while from the Admiralty we had requests for mooring buoys, large, flat floating tanks; and from Trinity House, orders for various types of marker buoys to mark both shipping lanes and the increasing number of dangerous wrecks around our shores. Each order had to be accompanied by the appropriate certificates, specifying the weight of steel and our place in the priority ordering queue. My job was to obtain these supplies for our workforce, many of whom had never before even seen the new lines they were designing and making.

At the outbreak of war there were quite a few shops near our office, tobacconists and confectioners, but gradually they closed down with the introduction of rationing. There was also a pawnshop, but the war meant plenty of work was available and earning a living became easier, legal or otherwise. Spivs flourished in the East End, forming a Mafia of their own.

DAD'S ARMY

In the spring of 1940, the rapid advance of the German Blitzkrieg caused a panic rush to join the Home Guard. Six of our men joined, and the headquarters in Bow Road was the factory of Ben Williams, who had a contract making uniforms for all the services, including the police. We had the best turned-out guards in the country! Fire guards, too, were organised, and a small bedroom-cum-canteen was set up for the four who would be on duty every night. Although we were paid ten shillings a night there were always defaulters, and I became a regular stand-in as I had to be in the building on a more-or-less permanent basis. It was agreed that we would spend our nights below ground, not only to protect ourselves against Nazi bombs, but against the fall-out from our own ack-ack – a wise precaution, as it happened. HMS *Kelly* and HMS *Cossack* were in dry dock, commanded by Mountbatten. One night, they opened fire on the bombers heading back from having another go at the Thames bridges. We heard the guns getting louder, then suddenly a shell landed, right in the middle of a delivery of steel pressings for a consignment of 500-gallon tanks for the Air Ministry. Fortunately the six-feet-high stack of metal stopped the sideways blast. As the manager responsible for reporting it, I could hardly classify this as enemy bomb damage: we had the end cap of the shell with the WD arrow mark still on it. The recoil of the gun knocked the ship off its props and it developed a 20-degree list. Someone must have been torn off a strip!

Headquartered at the factory of Ben Williams, uniform-maker in Bow Road, we had the best turned-out Home Guard unit in the country.

During the raids, I would emerge like a mole above ground and confer with our night watchman, to see if there was any damage to the buildings, which he guarded from his concrete hut. The windows were protected with plywood boards, which he put up every evening before the sirens went. His dog Sheila slept under the table in a wooden box with a blanket in it. He was without doubt one of the bravest men I have ever met, and a really wonderful worker, having been taken on after the First World War on his release from a German PoW camp. After we had exchanged information, he would walk home to Forest Gate, five miles away, and the following night, tell me everything he had seen along the way. Meanwhile, my bosses would telephone from their suburban hideaways to enquire if there had been any bomb damage to the factory, if any money had come in, any new orders taken or whether the War Office inspectors had been to check the previous orders, so that they could be released.

After a heavy raid one night, I answered the telephone to an anxious manager from the local Sanitas factory. He asked if I could send over some men with corrugated iron sheets to seal off the works, as a bomb blast had shattered the windows and blown in the doors. A team were duly dispatched to the site about two miles away and, in the evening, returned and gave me a detailed report of what they had done and the materials they had used for the job. Two days later, a man came into the office asking for me. He was from Sanitas, and I quickly explained that I had not yet made up the account and hoped that nothing was wrong with the job. He admitted that we had

The author, fourth from the right, centre, with a basket to collect up human body parts for identification and burial. It was a pitiful sight watching the homeless people scrabbling through the rubble for their few personal possessions.

made a very good job and would I thank the men, and ask them if they had seen six half-hundredweight boxes of soap, about three feet square? These were ready to be dispatched to the Army but had disappeared. I explained that our lorries were of the flatbed type, with no sides or covers, so nothing of that size could have been removed by my men. After he had gone, one of the office boys asked me if the man was from the CID; had he asked me for the names and addresses of the men I had sent to the factory, and had he asked me about soap? I told him off for listening in on my conversation.

Well, that night I had soap on my mind and in the morning, went to see the gang foreman to ask him what he knew about it. He immediately assured me that my share was underneath the bench in the garage. I guess that, if I had not asked, he would not have volunteered this news.

I took some of the soap home and gave it to Lucy, my mother-in-law, who was living with me at the time. She was highly pleased, soap being in short supply; at least, until she tried to use it, when her expression of pleasure changed to a scowl. The soap was hard as stone and, even with boiling water, she could not get it to lather. The 'perks of the job' were reluctantly consigned to the dustbin; our loss, though, was probably the Army's gain.

Londoners bed down for another night on the platform at Elephant & Castle underground station. Over 200 died in an escalator panic at Bethnal Green.

A remarkable news photograph of buildings collapsing in Queen Victoria Street at the height of the Blitz. The road was blocked and rescue workers had to go for miles around other bomb damage to get back to their depot.

SHELTERS

On a rare visit home to Dagenham I found Lucy distraught. The underground shelter that we had taken so much trouble to dig had filled with water almost to ground level. At that time, the firm obtained about five tons of cement and several thousand bricks and this was issued to the work force to protect their families. I mentioned the problem of the Anderson shelter to my boss, Mr Tawse, and between us, we designed an elaborate, reinforced steel shelter to be erected above ground. This protected my family through the years of near-misses and became a play cabin for the children after the war. But I could not keep in touch with the office from there. One day, a senior Naval Officer visited us to press for a large order of paravanes, a device towed by minesweepers, and I mentioned my problem to him. Within three days a pole was erected and our house became the only one in the street to have a telephone! The officer was later appointed to command a destroyer.

Not every household had a garden suitable for an Anderson shelter; such dwellings were issued instead with a Morrison shelter, a sturdy, table-like construction made of steel, capable of taking two or three people at a pinch, for indoor use. Hundreds of street shelters, too, were constructed of brick, topped with a reinforced concrete roof. They had strong steel doors and, in front, a blast wall to prevent a near-miss from buckling the door. Several of these shelters were built for the people who lived in the Poplar tenements known as 'the buildings', four-storey blocks of flats between the

The author's brother-in-law, Taff Eardley, is the lower figure on the ladder. Their job was to guide a steel hawser around the brickwork so that the building frontage could be pulled down, in case it fell on people on their way to work the next day.

Damage on the number 57 bus route at the corner of Poplar High Street and Cotton Street.

Blackwall Tunnel and Cotton Street, and several others on Mannisty Street. Many of the people living there took shelter in the tunnel at night, sleeping sometimes on the roadway when it was closed during raids. The tunnel had to be sealed off, as a direct hit could have caused serious flooding. Street wardens and sometimes even the police were on hand to keep the peace, in case of territorial squabbles. The crowded tenements in Whitechapel and Aldgate were occupied by the large Jewish community, overlooking their workshops and market stalls. They suffered tremendous damage and many personal tragedies. The children had been evacuated, but elderly and housebound occupants were trapped in the upper floors. Taff, my brother-in-law, was on Heavy Rescue duty and told me of the numbers of people he and his squad tried to save.

Further towards the City the underground stations made ideal shelters for thousands who slept on the platforms, arriving early to get the best spots. London Transport staff tried to keep the platform edges clear for the travellers. On 13 April 1943, I was on duty and went as usual to have breakfast in the Regent Café in Bow Road. The owner told me of a tragedy: 200 people had lost their lives at Bethnal Green station. I doubted this, as there had been no bombing incidents that night. Later, ARP headquarters told me there had been a rush to get in as the siren sounded. Someone tripped, people piled in behind, and hundreds were crushed to death.

As if on a film set, survivors gather together their few possessions in a street blasted apart by a V1 flying bomb.

Heavy raids on ports and factories came to a climax on 7 September, the 'Battle of Britain' as it became known. It started over London at about midday just as our workers were getting ready to go home. Everyone wanted to get transport out rather than stay in the shelters. As the train came in I was showered with brick dust and debris. As we left the station, there was a loud explosion. Through the windows we saw a huge blaze that marked the end of William Lusty Ltd, the factory that made Lloyd Loom furniture. It was one of the most memorable journeys I ever made. As the train arrived at each of the seven stations to Dagenham there were crowds gazing at the sky, where massed ranks of bombers flew in formation. When I got to my house, everyone was standing outside, cheering as the little Spitfires and Hurricanes weaved in and around this slow-moving target. Each victory was greeted with shouts and applause, as the bombers spiralled to earth, exploding in fields miles from their intended target, London's docklands. Even so, the damage was widespread and as it grew dark, the sky over the East End was livid and the air-raid sirens were wailing

Rescuers search the rubble of a bombed-out house where the collapsing roof has left a chance there might be survivors.

once more as another group of raiders arrived to harry the emergency services, an easy target lit by the burning buildings.

When I got to work the following Monday workmen were digging through a huge crater, all that remained of our underground shelter, which would have held most of our workers had they decided to stay.

A NEAR-MISS

Where we lived in Dagenham we had the May & Baker chemical factory near to one side of our home, and Ismay Cables and the Sterling Wireless building on the other. One night, the noise was unbelievable as a large number of bombs fell in succession, the explosions mingled with the pounding of the ack-ack. There was a prolonged whistle and a thunderous bang, followed by another three, coming nearer and nearer – then a break, and then a very large explosion seemingly only yards from our shelter. However, there was no follow-up blast or dust and debris that usually followed a building being hit, just a long vibration that shook the shelter and blew our candle

A young female survivor is pulled from the cellar of her house.

over, then darkness. Torches were quickly found and switched on. We could hear the sound of the retreating plane followed by the rapid-fire barking of the guns, each with twelve barrels all firing at the same time. No one was calling out, as neighbours did after a near-miss, to check that everyone was all right, and rescue workers would arrive at the scene to see if they were needed, but this time all remained quiet. Then suddenly we heard from next door: 'Blimey, John, that was close, I thought it was in your garden, it woke me up!'

The author is one of the group at the foot of the ladder, waiting to collect a box of spirits, a dog and a cat in a basket —
followed by the landlady of this pub in Shoreditch, who insisted on going back for the till takings before allowing herself to
be rescued from the second-floor window.

When daylight came we emerged to find that a stick of seven bombs had been dropped along the road, but one must have overshot and missed us out. He can't have been a very good bomb aimer either, because the factories to the right and left of us were unscathed. After 7 September the bombers moved off to attack Southampton, Bristol and other cities, and the job of clearing up began. Army and navy squads undertook the very dangerous work of clearing up dozens of unexploded bombs and pulling down dangerous buildings. If there was one fate worse than being instantly vapourised, it was being buried under tons of collapsing rubble. Unexploded bombs continued to be dug up for years after, and there must still be many buried under the Thames between Hammersmith and Southend.

AND MORE NEAR-MISSES

Of course, the attacks did not end there. On 29 December there was an attempt to wipe out London with firebombs, followed by the dreaded parachute mines that few people had heard of. The following day, huge fires were still burning and I went out to take Taff, my brother-in-law, and his men some rations. The crew had just got back to base and Taff dragged me off to Leadenhall Street to show me something. The street was cordoned off and dangling from the telephone wires was a parachute mine, swaying back and forth in the gentle breeze, about ten feet long and the diameter of a galvanised dustbin. Taff's squad had been working right underneath, oblivious to its presence. The bomb disposal squad was expected any minute. We moved well away from the area, directed by the man Taff had left in charge, as six naval personnel came with ladders and boards and defused the bomb.

Lilian and the girls had returned home after fifteen months as we had hoped the worst was over. The winter set in and we slept in the dining room, near the open fire. A raid began, and at about midnight we heard a deafening explosion, the shutters rattled but, as things then quietened down, we slept on. Lucy woke at the crack of dawn just as the all-clear sounded and went to the kitchen to make us all a cup of tea. Returning to the dining room she stopped in surprise and exclaimed, 'Good gawd, look at all your faces!'. We looked at one another, then burst out laughing.

We were all completely black with the soot that had been blown down the chimney. We had a job cleaning the house, and the ARP warden came by and reported that the bomb had landed in a potato field about 300 yards away. Later that morning I got a call at work. It was Lilian, to tell me that the whole estate was being evacuated. A huge parachute mine had been found in the field, about 30 yards from our front door. I got a lift home, to find that the Navy had arrived and disarmed it. We

A female ambulance worker hears the sirens going off.

persuaded them to hang on while a hasty whip-round was organised to buy those brave lads all a drink.

There was massive devastation in Poplar and other parts of the East End from these mines. Unlike bombs, whose blast was dissipated mostly into the ground, these had tremendous sideways force and there was no hope of surviving within a range of about 400 yards. Our mine in Dagenham must have landed in earth too soft to trip the fuse, otherwise we should have booked an early daytrip to Heaven. Testimony to their frequent use on London was the number of stories of nightdresses, blouses, knickers and underslips run up from the parachute silk. The children even had silk skipping ropes, although they frayed easily.

WOMEN AT WAR

The women of Poplar were, in my estimation, the backbone of London's defiance of Hitler's onslaught. Many had seen their young children off on the evacuation trains and their sons and husbands off to the war. They had then taken up full or part-time

Rearguard action: switchboard operators at work, their helmets and gasmasks at the ready.

jobs, often while looking after elderly parents, and were dealing capably with minor hindrances like ration books. Many of the elderly, of course, had memories of the Zeppelin raids and were reluctant to use the shelters.

We should never lose sight of the hardships the young mums suffered. Just staying and keeping their families healthy, with no National Health Service to fall back on. In some cases they had free medical care at work; otherwise, doctors wanted paying. A number took up evening duties. The Auxiliary Fire Service, or AFS girls, would do a shift at headquarters or go out driving supplies, often while the bombs were falling. In *Women Fire Fighters*, the ninety-five-year-old Cyril Demarne recognises their contribution; he was in charge of the Eastern region of London and I can vouch for many of the incidents he describes.

Then, there was the Women's Land Army, the WLA. In his book *War Time Women*, Michael Bentinck recalls from interviews the stories these marvellous girls passed on. We heard about them on the cinema newsreels and saw them in their uniforms when they paid a flying visit back from the countryside to homes and relatives in the East End. They looked rosy cheeked and healthy, but we never knew what hard work they performed in helping to keep us fed. Many farmers treated them as cheap slave labour, and they have not always had the credit they deserve.

The huge volunteer army of the WVS gave untold assistance to the ARP, Heavy Rescue, Fire service and police. These 'women in green' have been well written about in a book by Chas Graves. They were organised to reach bomb sites while rescue work was underway to give comfort to tearful survivors and workers alike, with cups of hot tea made on the spot to fortify them against the dreadful scenes and experiences and to be on hand until there were no more survivors to be found.

A WVS volunteer came across a little old man searching in the rubble of his home, pulling out some of his recognisable belongings. She offered him a cup of tea and a bun. He sat down on a stool he had recovered and drank the tea, but refused the bun. A short while later he wandered up to the van and she said 'Like a cup more tea?' and he replied, 'Can I have that bun now I've found my teeth?'

DOODLEBUGS

After four years of bombing there was delight and relief when we learned that the invasion had begun on the Normandy coast, with our Canadian and American allies. There was no possibility of repair work though, owing to the shortage of materials; besides, the residents were long gone. Poplar was a ghost town, piles of rubble everywhere with, here and there, a house that looked as though it had escaped destruction, until you looked more closely and saw that the rooms were all boarded up. With few customers and fewer goods to sell, it was a wonder any shops and factories remained open, but they did. Millwall was busy assembling and launching landing craft on the Thames slipway, and the famous Mulberry harbours that solved the problem of landing supplies behind the invasion forces, as no French deepwater ports had been captured. But it was a dreary place in the evenings when small groups of people made their way to huddle for the night in the shelters they found open.

At the time of the invasion, Hitler launched his secret 'vengeance weapons' on England. The first flying bomb to arrive was at Bow, in Grove Road. I saw it streak

A V1 'doodlebug' flying bomb, 1944/5. Hundreds of launch sites, known as 'ski' sites because of their curved shape, were hurriedly assembled in Holland and Northern France, pointing mainly to London, but the relatively inaccurate and slow V1 was soon to be superseded by something far nastier.

across the sky from Kent, and we all cheered, thinking it was an enemy plane shot down by the batteries furiously banging away on the other side of the river. Indeed, the BBC Home Service announced it in those terms the next day; that was all the Germans needed to hear. As they had lost no aircraft, they knew their V1 flying bomb, which soon came to be known by Londoners as the Doodlebug, had reached its target. There were many more to come.

Twenty-five feet long, loaded with jet fuel and one ton of high explosive, with only a rudimentary guidance system the V1 bomb relied on a precise measure of fuel to reach its target: when the engine cut out, you had just 15 seconds before it came down. Carried on lorries and trains they were easy to launch, and there were hundreds of sites around northern France and Holland. The south London borough of Croydon was particularly badly hit, as many fell short of their central and east London targets. In the space of three weeks, fifty-six landed on Croydon, demolishing 60,000 homes. In total, over 4,000 got past the RAF, ack-ack and barrage balloon defences to the London area, and poor old Poplar got thirty-nine to add to the tally of devastation from the Blitz. This campaign carried on for about nine months until, one by one, the Allied invasion forces closed down the sites. Without the heroism of RAF and USAF aircrew on constant bombing missions to disrupt the V-weapons supply trains, it might have been a lot worse; the miracle is that Hitler did not order the use of his chemical and biological warheads.

The V1s were fast and hard to shoot down, but pilots developed an interesting method of dealing with them, aided by the Tempest aircraft which arrived to replace the ageing Hurricanes and which was faster even than the Spitfire. They flew alongside

A very large bomb crater in Cottage Street.

Devastation at Devitt House, Wade's Place, Poplar, after an air raid in October 1940. Many elderly people were trapped in the upper floors of these tenement flats.

Right: A warden calls for assistance as the dog seems to have found something.

Below: Rigden Street, Poplar, after an air raid on 13 October 1940 in which four people were killed.

The King and Queen visited the East End, here on the site of The Eagle pub in East India Dock Road with the Mayor, Cllr Mrs Lilian Sadler and the head warden, Mr Cole. Princess Margaret is on the right and Princess Elizabeth has her back to the camera.

and used their wingtips to flip the 'doodlebug' off-course, hopefully to land harmlessly in the Romney Marshes. One New Zealand pilot was not so lucky, however; his plane collided with the V1 and he was killed, tragically as he was due to marry his WRAF officer sweetheart on the following Saturday.

Fortunately, Hitler then directed most of the V1 onslaught on to Antwerp, where the Allies now had the deepwater port they needed to unload supplies for the invasion forces facing counter-attack in the Ardennes.

After the V1 came the V2, a much more sinister and powerful guided rocket that weighed 13 tons and travelled at 3,000 mph. We owed a great debt to Miss Babbington-Smith, a WRAF reconnaissance officer, who first spotted the assembly and launch sites at Peenemünde on the Baltic, enabling the Allies to launch bombing raids against them. The first one to land was at Chiswick, and the BBC gave out details of a 'gas explosion' that did not fool anybody, least of all the Germans. We christened the V2 the 'Flying Gas Main', but it caused panic in the Government and despair among many Londoners. Was there no end to it?

Some colleagues and I narrowly missed becoming victims of one of these missiles. We had planned to meet up for lunch at the Cotton Street pub in East India Dock

The author's brother-in-law, Gordon 'Taff' Eardley, a City of London Heavy Rescue worker, leads a VE Day celebration goat-cart ride. He is seen in action earlier on page 99. The author's daughter Shirley, aged ten, with bow in her hair, watches her brave uncle from the background.

Road, a short bus ride from the office, but were late getting away and had to wait for another bus. Just before we reached the Blackwall Tunnel, we heard a huge explosion. Everyone was running, crying and shouting, many covered in glass, dust and blood. We felt a bit incongruous in our clean suits, staring at the pub and its surrounds, completely demolished, and bits and pieces of what looked like old clothes, but were in fact body parts, scattered around. There was nothing we could do there except get in the way, so we returned to the bus stop, pausing on the way to buy some 'lunch' from Mark's, a wonderful bakers I had known as a child. They fed us with buns and scones, and would not take a penny.

6

Friends & Neighbours

Having been born and lived in Poplar for twenty-three years, I was blessed with many friends. I have dedicated this chapter to the memory of family and neighbours who shared my boyhood, youth and young married life with me in Poplar, and then with my wife and her friends.

We lived at 19 Ida Street at first, and then crossed the road to the larger no. 20, leaving my brother and his wife at no. 19. Next to us at no. 17 was the Barnes family, my friend Albert, his sister Rosie and brother Jim. At no. 15 was the Pearce family, very hard-working and always poor. The son we loved was Stanley, who was in bad health. A lovely young man, he found work at the pawnbroker's to help the family purse. He did a good job on the repairs to our watches, that were always going wrong.

My father, his brothers and sisters, were born at no. 13 and lived there until my grandfather moved his haulage business to a large yard and house at Plaistow. Now, the Burgesses had the house, and they provided me with many hours of sanctuary, helping sometimes with their fruit shop. There were Norrie, Jimmy, Charlie, Lulu and Alfie, all looked after by their wonderful mother, Mrs Burgess, who was later described in Dorothy Scannell's book *Mother Knew Best* as 'a friend to all and one who listened and helped dozens of poor people in Poplar'. Norrie grew up and married a Mr Tucker and went to live in the house opposite. Alfie and Lulu were left in charge of the shop while Charlie, Jim and Mother ran the two stalls. I was always welcome in the kitchen and was treated as one of the family for many years.

On the opposite corner of Susannah Street was Storey's, the newsagents shop. You name it, they sold it – or could get it for you. Old Mrs Storey was an invalid who lived over the shop and was helped by her daughter, Mrs Sharp. She was the mother of my friend Sid. The shop was a real 'bush telegraph' exchange for all the local news and gossip. Waiting for Sid gave me an excellent opportunity to improve my education reading the lurid covers of all the comics and the latest Sexton Blake thrillers. Sid was a PoW in Germany during the Second World War; we corresponded right up until the end of the war and then we lost touch.

The George the Fourth pub was next along the pavement. The Darby family ran it with their daughter Hettie and young Steve, who was another of my friends, and their guard dog, an Alsatian called Wanda. The poor creature slept through not one but two burglaries! Next door, the Hall family were a homely lot; the youngest,

Every Monday morning there would be a queue of these women outside the pawnbroker's, or, as it says, the 'pledging department', ready to 'pop' their husband's best suit or a ring to buy food for the week until next payday.

The Revd A. and Mrs Tildsley introduced the author and friends to the magic lantern show and Felix the Cat at the Tabernacle on Thursdays after school.

another Sid, was a friend and we used the alleys around his house to dodge down and hide when playing chase. We also played the trick with a black string which had a cigarette packet attached to the end, cruelly 'catching' an elderly passer-by from the workhouse, one whose eyes were always on the ground.

Jack Emms the tailor was at the end of the street next to the East India Dock Road and on the opposite corner was the Jewish dentist, Mo Lewis, who kept goldfish and two parrots in his waiting room to amuse nervous customers. His yard was in Ida Street, and the Tates were the next along, friends of my brothers, who shared the same interests in dog and horse racing. The Frosts had a flat above the small shop called Dewberry's, Stan Frost was a member of our élite cowboy gang and later in the Army. He was sent to Calcutta, where he ran into my brother Steve one last time before Steve embarked on the Wingate expedition to Burma, from which he never returned.

Dewberry's was a lovely shop that I frequented when on errands for my mother and our neighbours, being nearer than St Leonard's Road or Chrisp Street. Sugar,

Poplar and Bromley Tabernacle ('The Tabby') was built in 1878 and destroyed in a 1941 air raid. The Revd Mr Tildsley was the minister from 1898 until 1945. Rebuilt in Brunswick Road in 1951, it was renamed the Poplar and Benger Baptist Tabernacle.

sold loose in blue conical bags, Zebra stove black, whitening for the doorsteps, Cross Brand tinned milk, flypapers, Sunlight soap wrapped in paper – they had the lot. The shop scales were used to weigh everything; everything smelt or tasted strongly of everything else. There was a sign above the till: 'No tick or slate'. The shop was on the corner of Follet Street, the home of some other friends of ours: the Rapsons, the Andersons, the Walters and the Coucha family, owners of the pease pudding and faggot shop in East India Dock Road. All their cooking and stewing was carried out in these back buildings and an aroma of excellence pervaded the street.

The other corner of Follet Street was the laundry with the ladies all working in a small area that could be seen through the windows. Mainly they worked with flat irons, pressing the laundry. On one side of the shop was the pick-up point for the new-fangled 'bag wash', where the van came round and collected washing for the Maxwell Bag Wash. This was frowned on by my mother and the hard-working women who did their own laundry in the backyard or used the public baths down the sideroad appropriately named Bath Street. The bags would be taken to an address in Peckham in South London and returned in a few days, all washed and paid for by weight. Of course, the washing was still damp and heavy and the owners had to dry and iron it themselves.

The Smiths and their neighbours were related to the Cann family. The younger Smith was enlisted in our gang. This was mainly because the lamppost was outside his house, and this was the initiation point for new members wishing to join. The

Mothers leaving the Council Relief Office, 1920s. Times were hard, and his disability proved a boon to the author's family when it came to 'deserving' food vouchers.

lamp was a welcome beacon for a card school or a spinning top competition with our Boxer peg tops. We always moved aside when the lamplighter came, with his long ignition pole.

The corner off-licence at the junction of Cook Street and Howard Street had a good following for their sweetshop trade, and our lovely friends the Thompsons had the first house along. She was a widowed lady, and her son John was a lifelong friend. Then came the Grimsdales, Irene – a friend of Lilian's – and her brother Ernie. They were next door to the Waters family, whose daughter worked with my brothers Harry and Ted in the Tea Pot Jones shop. She had two brothers, one a chemist's shop assistant who specialised in developing and printing films, the other a schoolfriend of mine. The Trenamen family were well known in the Poplar area, the father and son for their activities in the St John Ambulance brigade, a reassuring presence at theatres and football matches. Howard Street was the home of one of the first people in Poplar to appear on TV! Bill Morris was an accountant in the council rates department, a maths wizard who was challenged to a televised calculating race with a newly invented machine that worked on a chain-driven system – slow but accurate.

Kitty Mills was my schoolgirl pin-up. She lived with her sister Flossie and father George, who was one of the school governors. I had to escort him in the school as part of my duties. Next to us in our new home at no. 20 was the Faulkner family, a widowed mum and two unmarried daughters. They kept their backyard full of roses and had a steady demand for the plentiful horse manure. The long hedge of Virginia creeper that separated our gardens provided an abundant supply of caterpillars. The Stolleries lived at no. 22 next door; their only son commiserated daily with my brother on the failings of the various horses and dogs they backed. No. 24 was the home of Norrie Tucker, née Burgess, and her son Sam, who later played for West Ham. A tough character, he bore a long razor scar down his face, which was enough to frighten off most of his enemies.

Mr and Mrs Briggs lived at no. 28. Jack was an ambulance driver, a good-looking man who wore his cap at a jaunty angle and was admired by the ladies, but his wife was an angel. They had several children. Jack's yellow ambulance signified that a fever victim or suspect was on the way to isolation hospital and we children had strict instructions to stay away if it stopped anywhere near. The other ambulance he drove, a white one, meant an accident or emergency operation. Both had the big London County Council coat of arms displayed on the side.

On the opposite side with the odd numbers were Mr and Mrs Starling, a small, neat family with the hardworking husband a councillor in his spare time. He worked with the Relieving Officer, or RO, who was the man you went to see when the whole of Poplar was on the breadline and standing in all weathers outside the town hall hoping for assistance. Mr Starling had enormous compassion for all his neighbours. The Peaks lived next to them, and then the Wilsons and the Easterbrooks. Tommy Easterbrook was always effeminately dressed and put up with a lot of name-calling from the lads. He worked with a group of buskers, pulling a hired barrel organ along the streets. While the group did a tap dance, or turned the organ, Tommy would dance and sing and collectors passed the hat round.

Next to the Wilsons lived the White family. Their son Billy, an enterprising lad, courted our Lilian for a short while. His young sisters were a credit to the family; Mrs White dressed them in little starched pinafores over their dresses. The father was a merchant seaman, I believe. Then came the Mason's Arms, known as the Ash Bucket. The Smiths were our neighbours at no. 21. Their dad was one of the few who had a regular white collar job in one of the railway offices. He taught us children the basics of pigeon racing. We stood in the backyard, shaking the tin of feed to entice the birds to land in the lofts, where he would remove the small cylinders from their legs, then rush down the road to the punch-clock that recorded the race times. He bred Chow dogs, and showed them. We used to ask to see their tongues, which were naturally black. But they were not friendly dogs and we kept away from the fence when they were in the yard.

My brother George moved in at no. 19 when we moved out. I do not know if he was subsequently bothered by the ladies from the Ash Bucket. There were no conveniences in the pub and my mother, being a kindly soul, would let them in to use our outside loo. In nearby Grundy Street lived a number of friends of my family, the Bullocks, the Callaghans, the Ballards, who ran the bookstall in the market, the Shanks family, together with the Huckles and Pallets and the Murrays, who owned the Prince of

A view of Whitechapel High Street, c. 1910.

Wales pub. At the far end of Ida Street lived the Fennels, over the little general store that faced Hyams, the rag and bone merchants, with its ever-open door revealing a great pile of meat bones bleached and boiled dry and sold for coppers to buy the next meal. Hyams was never pleased with the rags you delivered, in common with most rag and bone men, who liked to haggle.

Deaffies, as it was known, was a dirty little shop. A deaf mute would take your order by having you write it on a slate. He sold coke, paraffin, firewood, carbolic and hauled the heavy sacks of coke on a barrow, right through the Blackwall Tunnel, the coke being cheaper on the other side than at the Leven Road depot. The Woolpack pub stood on the next corner, but Lilian and the family did not think much of the landlord, Mr Pye. He refused to telephone for an ambulance when Lilian was expecting our first baby, Shirley. He said it wasn't a public phone and I had to walk to the post office in the East India Dock Road, about half a mile from our house on Mauve Street. Word soon got around, and many customers chose to spend their hard-earned drinking money elsewhere.

The Edwards brothers ran the greengrocers on the corner of Burcham Street. They were a strange pair. When you went in and asked for potatoes, cabbages or the

other items they sold, you would give your order to one man, and the other would
come out and ask what you wanted. They were never apart and walked side by side,
in step, up and down the street like soldiers, although they were too old to have seen
service. Jona's was a handy little shop, a mini-general store and a godsend to mums
who ran out of the odd item. Sometimes we were served from the back door when
the shop was closed. Lilian's first paid job was running lunchtime errands for Mrs
Jona and again after school hours, after her mother's jobs had been completed.

Ada Humphries was a small, sweet lady who ran a little grocer's shop from the
rooms of her house. This was a little goldmine. Penny packets of tea, loose jam in
a cup and tins of condensed milk – a big notice on display, 'No slate or tick, refusal
sometimes offends, so do not ask.' This was at 6 Mauve Street. Next to her were the
Keefs, the Courtneys, the Rawlins and the Bridgens. On the opposite side were the
Sharps, the Gilberts, the Mancktelows, then Burcham Street, with Mr Colewick the
bookmaker and his mother, who sometimes lent money. Then came the O'Briens
and the Kidoza family, then the Ferries who worked at our local picture house, the
Pavilion. All were lovely neighbours, ready to help each other. All the time we lived
there we never heard a row or bad words between anyone; nor would you, anywhere
in the East End.

After leaving school I had little spare cash from my wages, and it was nice to know
there were so many pals you could meet without spending money. A short bus ride
and a long walk fitted the bill on most evenings and weekends. Susannah Street and
Lindale Street provided me with so many good times with the Fisher family, who all
had boxing and wrestling careers. Charley and Eddie fought under various titles on
the bills at Deptford, Mile End, Hackney and the upper-crust ring at Baker Street. Then
there were the sons and daughters of Mrs Briggs, the Chrisp Street flower lady, whose
stall was about 40 yards away. Eddie Briggs was a very good pal of Lilian's and mine,
he was a good trumpet player and was in several bands. He could play the piano and
croon in the Bing Crosby style, and the neighbours would be given a free rendering of
the latest hits as we were entertained in his front room.

His next-door neighbours, George and Billy White, were always willing to help
anyone. The Chrisp Street stallholders relied on them when trade became busy or a
refill was needed from the yards and lock-ups, and the market, where they earned a
small wage, was where we would usually find them. George Franklin was younger
than other friends in my circle; his admission had been purely an opportunity to get
to see and chat with his pretty sister, Dolly. The other two girls in Lindale Street were
the Fenners, two attractive young ladies who were ever the centre of attention of the
Bullock brothers. Another friendly and well-behaved young man I remember was Jess
Hill, who lived at the far end of Lindale Street. He and all the other mates, friends and
neighbours, we all came through the bleak days of poverty and hardship after the
First World War and the barren years that followed, into the 1920s. It always gives me
great pleasure to remember them.

For many years, before her last illness, Lilian too would recall happy times with
friends who were reliable and sincere. Her group of fourteen–eighteen-year-olds had
little spare time and in some cases were the eldest of a number of small ones who
needed looking after. They found comradeship and entertainment in the free evening
classes, however, encouraged by the London County Council. Among friends she

mentioned to me over the years were Ivy Green from Aberfeldy Street, Jenny Webb from Chilcott Street, Irene Grimsdale from Cook Street and Rosie Lindsey from Grundy Street, together with Rosie Freeman from the same area. She was particularly friendly with Joan Lovegrove, the daughter of the licensee at The Ellerthorpe Arms in Kirby Street. The Steggles from St Leonard's Avenue and the Hood family in Burcham Street were also mentioned. I am sure she would like me to mention all those lovely pals of Lily Morris from Mauve Street. A dear lady who comes to mind was one who lived opposite us, Mrs Donovan; she and my mother-in-law, Lucy Morris, grew up together with all the cares and worries of raising their families during those very hard times.

Reading through all the letters I have received while writing this book, I am astounded. The ladies, mums, wives and grandmothers all have very vivid memories of the days so long ago. They recall hundreds of incidents in their lives that had remained tucked away. It was a great joy to talk so many times with Becky Calnan (née Rapson), about the friendship of her brother Harry and how my mother treated him as one of the family. I have often been thanked for the recollection of an enjoyable time – but not so often for the hard times we all went through.